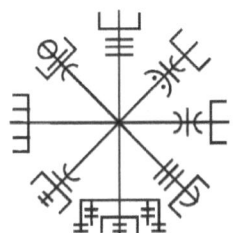

VEGVÍSIR

PUBLISHED BY AVALONIA LTD

ISBN: 978-1-910191-32-3 (PAPERBACK)

VEGVISIR: A PRACTICAL GUIDE TO RUNIC AND ICELANDIC MAGIC
COPYRIGHT CHRISTOPHER ALAN SMITH, © 2022

DESIGNED AND PRODUCED BY AVALONIA LTD
BM AVALONIA, LONDON, WC1N 3XX, UNITED KINGDOM
WWW.AVALONIABOOKS.COM

ALL RIGHTS RESERVED.

British Library Cataloguing in Publication Data. A catalogue record for this book is available from the British Library.

Every effort has been made to credit material to, and obtain permission from, copyright holders for the use of their work. If you notice any error or omission please notify the publisher so that corrections can be incorporated into future editions of this work. The information provided in this book hopes to inspire and inform. The author and publisher assume no responsibility for the effects, or lack thereof, obtained from the practices described in this book.

The reproduction of any part of this book, other than for review purposes, is strictly forbidden, in all formats, without the prior written consent of Avalonia Ltd and the copyright holders.

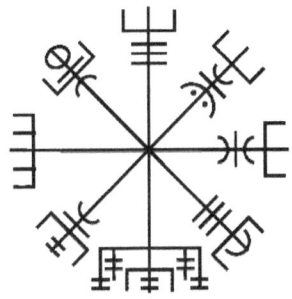

Vegvísir

*A Practical Guide
to Runic and Icelandic Magic*

Christopher Alan Smith

Published by Avalonia
www.avaloniabooks.com

For Laurie, Ranulph and Ingrid.

I wish to thank my wife, Laurie, for all her encouragement as I wrote this book. Thanks are also due to Kees Huyser for helping with the artwork, reading through the initial draft and suggesting the necessary corrections, and to Dave Lee for his encouraging comments after a preliminary reading. Last but not least, I thank the wonderful people at Avalonia, my publisher, for their patient work.

Christopher Alan Smith, June 2022

CONTENTS

Foreword 8

Introduction 11

PART 1:
PREPARING FOR THE MAGICAL LIFE

First Exercises 22

Taking it further 32

An Introduction to Rune-lore 43

Taking up the Runes 89

The Magician's Toolbox 99

Ritual Magic 108

PART 2:
THE TECHNIQUES OF RUNIC AND ICELANDIC MAGIC

Appeals to Supernatural Entities 122

Incantation 128

Runes and Bindrunes 131

Galdrastafir and Galdramyndir 137

The Methods of Delivery 154

Time and Space 160

Sendings 171

Divination 186

Washing Rituals and the Helm of Awe 194

A Sample Working 199

'Instant' Magic 206

APPENDICES

The Rune Gild 210

The Rune Rows 212

Of Málrúnir and the Rune-Kennings 219

A Brief Guide to the Gods, Wights and Worlds 226

A Select Compendium of Traditional Icelandic Spells 233

Bibliography 243

Index 246

FOREWORD

I began to write this new work on Old Midsummer's Eve, otherwise known as the Eve of St John's Mass – a magically significant date in the folklore of many countries, including Iceland and England – and I hope that this may prove propitious. It has now been over six years since my first book, "Icelandic Magic: Aims, tools and techniques of the Icelandic Sorcerers" was published, and it is high time that I gave heed to the many requests for a sequel, and to my own feeling that I had left much unsaid. My first book was a distillation of some five years of research into Icelandic magic as it was practised in the Early Modern Period. Apart from a few small changes, it closely followed the text of my Master-work for the Rune Gild, for which I was granted the title of Master in that organisation at Yule in 2014. In writing it, I was driven by *wōd* – that state of ecstatic inspiration which comes from Woden himself – and the words poured onto the paper as if they had a life of their own. Nevertheless, it was an exhausting process, which goes some way towards explaining why four years elapsed before I began this sequel. The book was well received in what is, after all, something of a niche market, and it gained many five-star reviews. While readers uniformly found it informative and highly readable, I noticed an unsatisfied demand for a more 'hands-on' approach, a book of practical instruction in the art of Icelandic magic. I pointed out that Dr Stephen E. Flowers had published, in the subsequent year, a book of exactly that type, but many people still wanted to hear it directly from me, and to know how I practise magic using the runes and the Icelandic *galdrastafir*.

This, then, is a response to that demand: an exposition of magic as I experience it and use it. It synthesises, in plain language and avoiding jargon as far as possible, over forty years of exploration, experimentation, exhilarating successes and - sometimes - bitter disappointments. Though primarily addressed to those who are complete novices in the magical arts, it may nevertheless offer something of interest even to advanced practitioners, if only for a difference of approach. It may stray at times from the core subject of Icelandic magic, bringing in customs from England or other countries; for this I make no apology, for I have nothing to prove in this work, no lofty status to seek. My one great hope is that readers will not only read it but also enjoy it, and use it wisely to improve their own lives and benefit mankind in general.

Christopher Alan Smith, 2022

A Note on Orthography and Pronunciation

This book occasionally uses Icelandic words and spelling. The Icelandic alphabet contains a number of characters that are not used in English. Furthermore, the pronunciation of vowels can be considerably changed by the addition of an accent over them. Here follows a brief guide to these characters and their pronunciation.

Þ   Pronounced with a hard 'th', as in 'thorn'.
Ð/ð Pronounced with a soft 'th', as in 'this'.
Æ/æ Pronounced as the English word 'eye'.
ö   Pronounced like the 'u' in the English word 'blur'.
a   As in British English 'man'.
á   As in the exclamation 'ow!'
e   As in British English 'men'.
é   An 'e' preceded by a 'y' sound, as in 'yes'.
i/y A short 'i', as in 'lift'.
í/ý A long 'i', pronounced as in 'magazine'.
o   A short 'o', as in 'cod'.
ó   A long, more rounded 'o', as in 'goat'.
u   A short 'u', as in 'but'.
ú   A long 'u', as in 'moot'.
ei Roughly as in English 'their'.
au Does not exist in English; best reproduced by pronouncing an open 'a' (as in the exclamation 'ah'), immediately merging into a closed 'u' as in French 'tu'. Somewhat similar to Dutch 'ui' but quite different to German 'au'.

Please note also that god-names and the names of the nine worlds are mainly rendered in their modern English versions in order to facilitate indexing.

INTRODUCTION:
WE, THE FORGETFUL DEMI-GODS

Throughout the ages, humankind has been plagued by fear and uncertainty. It is true that at some points in history - times of war, famine or plague - genuine uncertainty has prevailed, and there have been good reasons to be fearful. Times of great social, economic and technological change also cause anxiety when communities are disrupted, working conditions deteriorate, and technological advances bring benefits to a few at the expense of the majority. Such was initially the case during the Industrial Revolution of the 19th Century. Yet even in times of prolonged peace and plenty, we humans still have a talent for finding things to fear and reasons to be unhappy. We worry about our food, our weight and our health. We worry about crime. We watch the evening news with a mixture of outrage and despair. We view with astonishment the antics of our elected leaders. We curse our electronic windows on the world when they do not function as we wish and, when they do, we dive into the social media to whine and complain about all the aforementioned topics. Another cause of our discontent is that we are profoundly alienated from the kind of world that we were designed for. Working for a big corporation in a clerical role or on a production line can rarely be as satisfying as seeing the seeds you planted grow into crops and harvesting those crops, or having the skill to make a finished product all on your own. There is also an abrupt disconnection between the tools we use for business or entertainment and our capacity to make them for ourselves. Like our ancestors, we could – if we had to – learn to make an earthenware cup, a stone tool or even an iron knife, but a complex electronic device? No. Worse still, incessant advertising and marketing train us to believe that we can fill the void in our lives by acquiring more 'stuff', and that happiness is just around the corner with the next gadget;

we are constantly seduced away from the really worthwhile things because these do not generate cold, hard cash.

Such observations are not new, of course. They have been expressed by the artists, composers and writers of the Romantic movement, by William Morris and the Arts and Crafts Movement, and even by Charlie Chaplin in his film *Modern Times*. Technology may feed our bellies and cater for our material needs, but it does not feed the soul. Alas, neither does organised religion, although that is ostensibly its purpose. For millennia (or at least for the many centuries since the desert faith was imposed on our ancestors), the Abrahamic religions have solemnly sought to impose rules of behaviour that deny our human nature[1] and generally suck all the joy out of life. In return for good behaviour, they promise us, if we are good and obedient boys and girls and put up with everything life can throw at us, then we are allowed into a dreary afterlife in which there are no tears, hunger or sickness, thereby also depriving us of the joyful opposites of these and of all the challenges that used to make life interesting. Anyone questioning such a futile arrangement is told to have Faith (whatever that means), to refrain from questioning 'The Book', and to fear an alternative afterlife of everlasting agony. Some also argue that a utopian political solution is necessary, involving a better distribution of wealth and a much wiser (and usually much more oppressive) system of governance. The problem with utopian political solutions is that, like evangelical religions, they rely on the possibility of changing human nature by decree, and also rely on the assumed benevolence and altruism of the governors. Never have they worked out in practice.

Perhaps our discontent goes to a deeper level still, when something, a spark deep in our very being, whispers to us that our world does not have to be this way. That spark whispers of a time when it was a mighty flame that filled us, overflowed, and shaped the world around us. It reminds us

---

[1] Except, ostensibly, for the aspect of human nature that loves to violently inflict our religious tenets on 'unbelievers'.

that we have become lazy and complacent, and goads us to rebel against the passive, powerless role imposed upon us by centuries of organised religion and scientific rationality. When we hear this ancient, inner voice, we begin to remember who we really are, and some, the *best* of us, take heed. We start to take note of those times when we knew, without a doubt, that something was going to happen, even though we had no rational way of knowing it; the times when a fervent wish, backed by strong emotion, brought about the desired result; and we build upon these experiences, collecting and refining them, and work out ways that allow us repeat them at will. We realise that, armed with the right knowledge and with diligent training of mind and body, we can *change the story that we are living out* instead of being lowly actors in someone else's play. In his book "The Occult", Colin Wilson wrote:

> *"Suddenly I am aware of vast inner spaces of strange significances inside me. I am no longer a puny twentieth-century human being trapped in his life-world and personality. Once again, I am at the centre of a web, feeling vibrations of meaning... I am like a tree that suddenly becomes aware that its roots go down deep, deep into the earth. And at this present point in evolution, my roots go far deeper into the earth than my branches stretch above it – a thousand times deeper. So-called magic powers are part of this underground world: powers of second sight, pre-vision, telepathy, divination. These are not necessarily important to our evolution; most animals possess them, and we would not have allowed them to sink into disuse if they were essential. But the knowledge of his 'roots', his inner world, is important to man at this point in evolution, for he has become trapped in his image of himself as a thinking pygmy. He must somehow return to the recognition that he is potentially a 'mage', one of those magical figures who*

> *can hurl thunderbolts or command spirits. The great artists and poets have always been aware of this. The message of the symphonies of Beethoven could be summarised: 'Man is not small; he's just bloody lazy.'*"[2]

For we are, in fact, demi-gods at the level of mythic reality, and ours is the power to change and shape our lives, should we choose to do so. All we need to do is remember.

The Nordic Myths of Creation and the Origin of Mankind

Remembering starts with recalling and reinstating our ancestral myths. The word 'myth' is frequently interpreted these days as a false or fanciful story but, in reality, the role of myths is to convey a profound truth in a symbolic and metaphorical way. They are the *primal narrative*, the narrative that sets the tone and pattern for all other narratives. All cultures throughout time have had their creation myths, and the peoples of Iceland and Scandinavia are no exception. We are fortunate that theirs was committed to writing in the *Völuspá* (Prophecy of the Seeress), *Hávamál* (Words of High One, or Odin) and *Rígsþula* (Lay of Rig) sections of the Poetic Edda, and elaborated on in the Prose Edda of Snorri Sturluson. Were it not for these sources, we would be much the poorer; if the Germanic peoples elsewhere in Europe had similar creation myths of their own, these were eradicated and forgotten after the Saxons and Angles of England converted, and after Charlemagne's imposition of Christianity on the continental Germans. In summary, the myth runs as follows.

In the beginning, there was only Ginnungagap, the primaeval void. Two worlds came into existence on either side of Ginnungagap. To the north was Niflheim, a dark world of fog and ice, and to the south Muspelsheim, a bright and fiery world. Over aeons, these two began to close together across

---

[2] Colin Wilson, "The Occult", Mayflower Books, St Albans, 1973.

Ginnungagap. As the hot and flaming sparks flew from Muspelsheim, they met the freezing ice of Niflheim, causing a mighty explosion of steam. Eventually, the steam settled, condensed and froze again, forming shapes as hoar-frost forms from the freezing fog on a cold morning. One shape was human-like, but unimaginably vast and brutish: this was the frost-giant Ymir, and he spontaneously generated the race of giants, or Etins, from the sweat of his armpits and the mating of his own toes. Another shape was Auðumla, the cosmic cow, and from her udder Ymir drew his sustenance. Auðumla, in turn, looked around for something to eat and found a block of salty ice to lick. As she licked away at the block, a man-like figure began to emerge from it; this was Buri, the forefather of the gods. Buri must have mated with an Etin (though her name is not known), for he sired Borr who, in turn, mated with the Etin Bestla and sired three sons: Odin, Vili and Vé. These three sons abhorred what they perceived as the chaotic nature of their Etin-kin, and plotted a drastic takeover. Together they slew Ymir, their own maternal forefather; his blood issued in a great flood that drowned most of the Etins (though one named Bergelmir managed to save himself and his family). Then Odin, Vili and Vé took the corpse of Ymir, broke it into pieces and reassembled these to make Midgard, the Middle-enclosure. To the east of this, they gave a home to the remaining Etins, and below it they made Svartalfheim as a home for the Dwarf-folk, or Dark Elves. Taking sparks from Muspelsheim, they made the stars, the sun and the moon, and set them on their paths. Later, the three brothers were walking along the seashore in Midgard when they spied two logs, one of ash and the other of elm. The brothers[3] made the first humans, Ask and Embla, out of them. One gave them breath; another gave them inspiration, and the third gave them life and comely appearance.

---

[3] Named Óðinn, Hænir and Lóðurr in this passage, but ostensibly the same divine brethren.

> *"From the host came three mighty and powerful Aesir, to coast. There they found an ash and an elm of little might, and lacking orlog[4]."*

Then Odin, desirous of wisdom, wanted to know more about the nature of all things. He and his brothers had overturned the previous state of affairs, but he did not yet understand the multiverse that he had created. He had put much into order according to his own will, but just as much seemed to come from outside his own will as from within it. For example, he perceived that a great tree had grown, and that it held within its bole, roots and branches much of what he had generated, and much else besides. It seemed that he had been driven on by something outside of himself, and he wanted to know what these forces were. So badly did he want to have this knowledge that he felt he had to make an offering – but to what? After all, he was the architect of this multiverse. Therefore, he had to offer himself unto himself, to give his own life without stint in exchange for the knowledge. Selecting a sturdy branch of this mysterious tree, he attached a rope with a noose and put the noose around his neck. Kicking off into space, he also took a spear and thrust it into his heart for good measure. Bleeding, choking and dying, he descended into death, and the runes were revealed to him. He took them up, into himself, and with a great cry he fell from the tree and returned to life.

Having gained knowledge of all the runes, Odin gained even more power, wisdom and prestige. Each word led to another word, each deed to another deed. However, he wished to gain more knowledge still. At the foot of Yggdrasil, near one of its roots was the Well of Mimir, and this was said to be the source of much wisdom. Odin asked Mimir for a single draught from the well, but Mimir would not give this without something in exchange; Odin pledged one of his eyes,

---

[4] Völuspá verses 17-18, translation by James Allen Chisholm. 'Orlog' is akin to 'fate'.

which he tore out and cast into the well. He was then allowed to drink from the well of wisdom.

There was a being named Kvasir, who was created from the saliva of the Aesir and Vanir, the two families of gods, after they had made peace following their great war. He was most wise, and was said to be able to answer any question that was put to him. He was killed by two dwarfs, and they drained his blood and mixed it with honey to make the Mead of Poetry which they stored in three vessels called Boðn, Són and Óðrerir. This mead eventually came into the possession of a giant named Suttung, who set his daughter Gunnlöð to guard it in a hollow mountain. Odin heard about this mead and wanted it for himself. Using magic, he gained access to the cave, seduced Gunnlöð, and persuaded her to give him three draughts of the holy mead; he drank the contents of all three vessels, turned himself into an eagle and flew away with it to puke it out into other vessels when he reached Asgard. From this, he became the god of poetry, and dispenses some of the mead to those humans who are worthy to be poets.

Odin also gained great knowledge of all things past and to come by consulting a seeress (völva). Among other things, she foretold the death of Baldur and the coming of Ragnarök, the twilight of the gods. He also fared far and wide to pit his wisdom against other beings, such as Etins, and to gain more knowledge by questioning them.

Though he gives some of the mead of poetry to a favoured few, it is not recorded that Odin imparted his knowledge of the runes directly to mankind. That task fell to the god Heimdall in the guise of Rig. Rig moved for a while among the various classes of humans – thralls, yeoman farmers and warrior aristocracy – and lay with their women, sowing the seed of the Aesir among them. The son he sired among the warrior aristocracy, Jarl, grew to manhood and had the makings of a great king. Later, Rig returned to meet his son, taught him the Runes, and gave him his name.

> *"Then Rig came walking from the grove.*
> *Walking Rig came, taught him the runes*
> *and granted his own name,*
> *saying it belonged to his son. Rig bade him take*
> *possession of odal vales and old halls.[5]"*

Jarl waged war, gained territory, prospered and had many sons. His youngest son, Kon, was the best versed in runes:

> *"But young Kon knew the runes –*
> *age runes and life runes,*
> *and more to help pregnant women,*
> *some to blunt edges and some to calm the sea.*
> *He understood the chirping of birds, he quenched*
> *fires, calmed the seas, and soothed sorrows.*
> *He had the strength and endurance of eight men.*
> *He contended in runes with Earl Rig.*
> *He battled him in wits, and knew the runes better.*
> *So he came to have for himself*
> *the name Rig, and runelore.[6]*

In these Nordic myths, unlike in the Judeo-Christian tradition, the basic material from which humans are created is not inorganic dust but organic wood – the logs of ash and elm that were found on the sea shore. This shows to us that we are not mere mud-men, clay poppets shaped for the amusement of a capricious god. The Prose Edda abounds with kennings – metaphors – that describe humans as trees, demonstrating our kinship with living Nature as a whole. Furthermore, the god Heimdall (as Rig) copulates with the females of the three human classes and impregnates them with the divine seed. Mythically speaking, therefore, we humans are partly descended from a god. Mortal we may be, having a finite lifespan, but we are demi-gods nevertheless. And the best of us – but only the best, mind – become aware of this, are

---

[5] Rígsþula verse 35. 'Odal' is a concept of land by right of inheritance.
[6] Rígsþula verses 42-44.

reminded of it by the gods, are goaded to offer self to Self, are given the holy runes and a draught of the Holy Mead.

Not one in a hundred people will buy this book. Of those who do, not one in a hundred will read it through, understand its precepts, and put them fully into practice. Will you be one of the few? Will you remember?

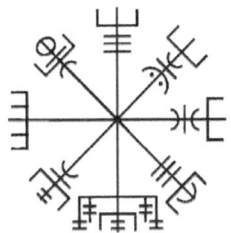

PART 1: PREPARING FOR THE MAGICAL LIFE

CHAPTER 1

FIRST EXERCISES

As you are reading this book, it is highly likely that you already have a strong interest in magic, or at least do not altogether discount its existence and effect. You are probably already practising magic to a greater or lesser degree, or have attempted some magical operation before, whether successful or not. Even if you think you have never consciously performed a magical act in your life, you probably have anyway. Have you ever expressed a hope or intention, and then said "Touch wood" (even without actually touching a piece of wood, as many do)? If so, you are evoking a benign wood-spirit to counteract any malign wight which might have heard what you said and resolved to thwart you. Do you cross your fingers when you want something to happen? Then you are evoking the Need-rune, of which more will be said later. My grandmother would never wash blankets in May, saying "If you wash blankets in May, you'll wash one o' t' family away". There are any number of such small acts and taboos, collectively termed 'superstitions'. I tend to collect these; though I do not actively go looking for them, they seem to come to me and, on the whole, they appear to work. If I can view the waxing Moon (before First Quarter) without seeing it through glass, and I bow three times and turn my money around, I know that I am going to have a good month. Regrettably, superstition is frequently conflated these days with stupidity and gullibility, but it is actually at the root of folk-magic everywhere. When superstitions and ancient lore are not learned from our forebears, as is increasingly the case, they tend to invent themselves in the form of urban legends, spontaneously arising in various, disparate locales, and then being propagated via social media and the more sensational press sources. The problem here is that the new urban legends, unlike the old lore, mainly feed on fear and do not include the necessary prohibitions and apotropaic actions. This can only be restrictive, so it is imperative that we open our minds to magic, learn the old lore, develop new lore appropriate to the 21st Century, and learn to exploit our inherent abilities, as sons and daughters of Rig, to make things happen according to our will.

Belief in magic has been ubiquitous throughout the ages, though perceptions of its nature and how to deal with it have varied from century to century and from culture to culture. In Europe, and in those colonies which were strongholds of transplanted European culture, it suffered a setback during the Age of Enlightenment (roughly 1700 to 1800 CE), when a philosophy based on the sovereignty of reason and the evidence of the five bodily senses not only challenged the old political and religious order, but also declared belief in magic irrational, and its practice impossible. The Enlightenment gave rise to great scientific progress, furthered the cause of individual liberty, and promoted the concept that government should be based on just and rational rules. It also had the fortunate effect of terminating the vicious persecution of people for witchcraft (whether real or imagined) which had prevailed - mainly in the Protestant countries - throughout the previous century. However, its dry insistence that all things must be measured and attested by the five bodily senses failed to feed the requirements of the soul or to explain the common human experience that some events and abilities are simply uncanny, difficult to quantify, and hard to consistently reproduce. Resistance to the orderly, scientific rationality of the Enlightenment led first to the Romantic movement in the first half of the 19th Century and subsequently to the Occult Revival, which began in the latter half of that century and has continued since.

In European culture, magic and its practitioners (with a few notable exceptions such as John Dee and Heinrich Cornelius Agrippa) have mostly been considered somewhat disreputable and outside of 'normal' society. Among the common folk, magic was both feared and respected, while established religious structures - even in pre-Christian, Imperial Rome - resented the challenge to authority that it represented. Today, a bald statement that one is a magician will elicit a mixture of responses[7]. Some will assume that you are an ignorant crackpot (a relic of that Enlightenment-age 'scientific empiricism'). Others may fear and shun you, or ask whether you can get rid of warts[8] or, mistaking you for a stage conjurer, ask whether you can pull a rabbit from a top hat. While it must also be admitted that the modern occult scene has its share of frauds, ego-trippers, pathologically disputatious people and quite a few who are probably certifiably insane (so choose your company carefully), many are highly intelligent, well-educated, rational and gifted people. They have simply seen beyond the narrow, Enlightenment-age outlook that if something cannot be measured or consistently repeated, it does not exist. Working from an inner instinct that there must be more to the Universe than bland, mechanical cause and effect, they began to experiment with magic and found that it works. Not all the time, admittedly, but with practice it can be made to work more often than not.

The popular conception of the magician has traditionally fallen into one of two categories. The first conceives of the magician as a person with a natural talent (frequently based

---

7 Immediately after writing this, I saw a headline in the 'Daily Mail': "Woman accidentally stumbles across a meeting of SATANIC SEX CULT members clad in black robes on her way to the toilet at a vegan café" Some things never change!
8 You can. This was, I think, my very first conscious act of magic. I was 20 years old, a student in Sheffield, and I had multiple warts on my right hand. Using the lore taught to me by my grandparents, I asked a local butcher for a small piece of meat. "What do you want it for?", he asked. "To cure a wart", I replied. Without batting an eyelid, he cut off a piece of meat of about one square inch, wrapped it and gave it to me, refusing payment. Later that day, under the Full Moon, I rubbed the meat on the warts and then buried it in soil. Within 3 weeks, all the warts had disappeared.

on heredity) for performing certain wonders such as healing or cursing, requiring little or no formal tuition. The second category conceives of the magician as a person of average natural talent who, by dint of apprenticeship lasting many years to an established master, develops his or her 'occult' abilities far beyond the usual measure. In practice, the truth is that natural talent must be constantly refined, exploited and subjected to disciplined training to make its mark. In any sphere, the person of average talent who diligently trains and exercises will generally out-perform the naturally talented person who does nothing. My view is that all humans have a latent ability to perform magic, but most restrict themselves due to fear, laziness and lack of self-confidence.

There is always a price to pay. Not in loss of sanity or in the form of some diabolic pact (unless you choose to go down that route), but simply in terms of some hard work on yourself. In order to practise magic, you will need to develop those personal skills that have hitherto lain unused, and to open up your mind to a host of new possibilities. You will also have to break away from some established, habitual behaviour and develop new habits. It does help to have someone more experienced to coach you along the way and, in that respect, I highly recommend the Rune Gild for its well thought-out learning programme and the possibility to apprentice oneself to a Master[9].

Changing the Narrative

This is, I hope, the only point at which I may have to disappoint and disillusion the reader. If you are expecting the kind of magic which features in popular fiction - hurling thunderbolts, levitation, psychokinesis etc. - then you need to rethink things. I am not saying that such things are not possible; after all, it is better to keep an open mind, and I have heard some creditable accounts of such occurrences from other magicians; but when they occur, they often happen

---

9 See Appendix 1 for more information.

spontaneously and tend to surprise the magician as much as anyone else. Various attempts have been made to define operative magic. Michael Kelly, in "The Book of Ogham", defines it as: "A technique by which a human being is able, by the power of volition, to affect events in subjective and/or objective reality, which given ordinary means would be impossible." In other words, it is the art of changing things, situations and perceptions by acts of focused will. Although such acts do not accomplish their ends by the 'normal' physical, chemical or biological means, they nevertheless work in harmony with the laws of Nature. In "Circles of Power", John Michael Greer gives a hypothetical example of trying to move or levitate a stone by means of a magical ritual. Common sense tells you that the stone is not simply going to fly; stones just don't do that unless propelled by some other agency. However, you may be able work things so that a passing small boy picks up the stone and flings it, *by coincidence*.

Personally, I think of magic as the art and science of changing the Narrative[10]. Narrative is not just a matter of idly telling stories; it is a powerful force in its own right, exerting itself through mythic reality, in ancient folktales, and in the story you tell yourself, day in, day out. Some narrative themes have such power that we can find ourselves reliving a 'fairy tale', step by step, especially when another significant person in our life knows the same tale and, consciously or not, plays it out with us. In Nordic mythology, our fates are determined at birth by the Norns, whose names are Urð, Verðandi and Skuld, which respectively have the meanings of 'what has become', 'what is becoming (now)' and 'what should become (in the future)'. *What has become* - also known by the Old English name of Wyrd - is the most solid of the three. She represents all the deeds and actions of the past which form and bind you. For example, if you are born into a lowly family

---

10 "Changing the narrative" has become something of a buzz-phrase these days. All too frequently, it has been cheapened in practice to mean 'spin' and Orwellian Newspeak - in other words, lies. Here you get the real deal.

with a poor reputation, it is likely that you will find it difficult at first to make headway, as you lack financial resources and are judged on the basis of your family's reputation, however hard you try. Verðandi, *what is becoming*, is a single, ever-moving point in the timeline of your life. She relates to everything that you are doing right now, and everything that is going on around you at this moment, where 'now' is constantly turning into 'what has become' and being replaced by a new 'now'. Verðandi may seem ephemeral, but she is crucially important. The decisions and actions taken today will become, and add to, your Wyrd. The third Norn, Skuld, says what should become in the future, based on what has happened in the past and what you are doing right now. Not *shall* become, mind, but what *should* become; it is conditional, and depends on decisions, actions and influences which still lie ahead. Skuld's name is also related to 'Schuld', the Dutch and German word for 'debt'. The future is in debt to the past. If you take out a loan, you will have to repay it in the future, or take the consequences. On the other hand, it may lie within your power *now* to gain the means for repayment so that it falls lightly.

Every day, we live within our own narrative and, all too often, reassert it even when it is a negative one. You can see it all the time on social media: "I am sick"; "I am poor"; "I am in an abusive relationship". What people seem not to realise is that they are creating and maintaining this for themselves and reinforcing the unhappy circumstances in which they find themselves. They are writing a bad Narrative. I was once in such a situation. I was in a job that I hated. I had expected that it would be my dream job, but it brought a lot of responsibility and stress that I could not handle. I used to wake up in the morning and dread the prospect of going to work and the day that lay ahead. Until, at a certain moment, I realised that this was a very unhealthy approach and decided to turn things around. After all, there were so many positive things in my life as well. I had a decent salary. I had a loving and supportive wife. I had my health. And, above all, while there was breath in my body, there was hope and the opportunity to turn things around. So, instead of dreading the day ahead, I opened the curtains and said aloud "Thank you, mighty gods, for this day you have given me!" And then I took everything that the day could throw at me with a light heart and a sense of humour. If I failed at some things, it did not matter as long as I had done my best. Furthermore, I started to look for positive solutions to the predicament that I was in, and found them, eventually leaving the company and becoming self-employed.

Consider, also, the extent to which your personal narrative and perceptions are influenced by exposure to the mainstream press and the social media. The dictum of the mainstream press is that bad news sells, good news does not, so we are bombarded by stories of climate change, ecological catastrophes of other types, war, dreadful accidents, corruption and social inequality. It is all designed to bring you down and keep you sad or outraged. Ask yourself: Where does this get me? How much influence can I really exert on these things? How much effort am I really prepared to put into changing them, given my personal priorities? The answer, given due and sober consideration, is probably "Not very much". So why do you follow all this negativity? Examine your own life. There are probably some aspects of it that you would wish to change. Magic can help you to do this, but it helps to approach things with a positive frame of mind. Having all the word's misfortunes dumped under your nose every five minutes is not going to foster this attitude.

Mythic narrative is not a tale of things past. It plays itself out time and again, over and over. Consider Ginnungagap, the magically charged void that is empty and yet filled with infinite potential. That is, in fact, where we all find ourselves at the start of every new day. In every infinitesimal moment, even. If we don't realise that and make a conscious and wilful decision to take and shape the material that is at hand, the void will become populated anyway by shapes, beings and forces that we do not consciously evoke. These take on a life of their own and often entice us into playing their game, pursuing a lazy fantasy. If we are unwise, we can even allow these entities and forces to control us, labouring under the illusion that this is reality and that we are powerless to fight against it or to take another course. Odin and his brothers, Vili and Vé, were the first to realise this, even before time came into being. They were born into a universe (for want of a better word) populated by the primaeval and chaotic race of giants, but they slew the progenitor of the race of giants and used his substance to create seven of the Nine Worlds according to their own design. Later, the gods created the race of mankind, sowed their own divine seed in that race, told their story, imparted many runes and gave us the ability to seek Rúna, the Great Mystery. For better or worse, most of humankind have forgotten their divinity and are now in thrall to the basest aspects of the World-forces, forgetting (if they ever knew it) the prime example of Odin. People grumble but they do not seek, and when their bellies get too empty, they lash out with unthinking force, blindly, against the first perceived source of their woes. Better it is to be aware, to make the best of the opportunities of the moment (without getting entirely caught up in illusion) and to plan - carefully, quietly and decisively. For the magician, there is no 'reality'; there is only the Narrative. It is not illusion. On the contrary, it is very real, and it can make your life heaven or hell, or something of a combination of the two (which is what most magicians prefer, as an eternity of one or the other would become very boring indeed). The trick lies in realising that, while Narrative can shape you, you can also shape the Narrative. You decide, quite simply, that the story should be told differently and have a different outcome to what was expected. All the rest is a matter of practice and, yes, it can require arduous and diligent self-training and learning of the techniques, but at the heart of it lies the conviction that you can turn things around. To really make it work, you have to discover what it is that you really want.

EXERCISE 1

<u>Start writing a magical diary</u>. This is going to be your work-book, your grimoire, and the tale of your deeds, so acquire the handsomest blank notebook that you can afford. If you cannot afford much, no matter; use a cheap, simple exercise book of the type you probably used at school. Begin by describing your present situation as a series of bullet-points:

- Your strengths;
- Your weaknesses;
- Aspects of your life which you enjoy and wish to conserve or enhance;
- Aspects of your life which you dislike, and wish to change or eliminate.

Look at all of these calmly and dispassionately. This personal analysis will form your baseline, to which you can refer in the future in order to assess your progress. Above all, be honest with yourself, and forgiving of your perceived failings. After making this initial analysis, record your exercises and magical deeds every day, even when you feel you have done nothing special. If you have not stuck to your daily exercises, for example, think about why and how that happened, so that you can remedy that problem henceforth.

EXERCISE 2

<u>Positive Daily Assertion</u>. Every day, on waking, give thanks for the new day, and celebrate the fact that you live and breathe. Push away all negative thoughts and fears. Take a deep breath and see yourself as being in control, the arbiter of your own fate. Formulate an assertion on the lines of:

"Thank you, mighty Gods, for this new day!
I give thanks that I live and breathe!
This day will be a good day!"

This is just a suggestion, and you can formulate it differently as long as everything you declare is positive. If you are not a polytheist, you can substitute some other 'higher power', whether that be God, Jesus or simply the Universe. Make this your daily habit. If you have been in the habit of tumbling out of bed and rushing to get ready for work, then stop! After all, how long does it take you to make this assertion? Only a few seconds.

EXERCISE 3

<u>Ginnungagap</u>. On waking, and after making your Daily Assertion, take one minute to tell yourself the narrative of the day ahead. Shape it, picture it, and tell it to yourself, as if it had already happened. In doing so, shape your world to be as you wish it to be; do not manifest your fears!

EXERCISE 4

<u>Retrospective</u>. At the end of the day, as you prepare to sleep, reflect on the day's events as they happened. In recalling them, it helps to work backwards from the end to the beginning. How do you feel about the way the day turned out? How did it compare with the way you shaped it in the 'Ginnungagap' exercise? What lessons have you learned?

These four exercises should form part of your daily routine from now on. Give yourself a week to get used to them before adding more exercises. Remember to maintain daily diary entries to keep an account of your progress, also noting any unusual changes in your life, dreams etc.

CHAPTER 2

TAKING IT FURTHER

Great. By now, you should be noticing some changes in your life and in your attitude to it. For some, this may already have brought about such a positive difference that it is as far as they want (or need) to go. If so, that is fine, but you are not yet practising magic. Remember that you are born a demi-god, and that amazing power lies within you. You have started on the journey and, with more effort, you can bring about even greater changes in your abilities. To do this, you will need to find a little more time in your day. "But I am already so busy!", I hear you protest. Consider this: how much time do you spend flicking through the social media, the news and other internet sites, watching inane TV shows, or exchanging gossip at work? Try logging it: I bet it will easily come to several hours per day.

All I am asking of you is that you find 20 minutes in each day to genuinely focus on improving yourself and bringing out those awesome, god-like abilities. Even if you are a single, working parent, I bet you can find those 20 minutes if you really want to; perhaps in two 10-minute sessions if it has to be that way. This chapter will introduce new exercises that will feel hard at first, but will pay great dividends. It is better than a subscription to the gym, as it will not cost you a penny!

Meditation

Now I really hear you groan. Perhaps you have tried it before. It can feel like being stuck in the 'naughty corner' to review and repent your sins, when all your friends are having a great time and getting on with the lesson that 'teacher' has laid down. So let's turn it around. 'Teacher' is now the dazzling ball of deception and distraction presented by modern life. You need a rest from this in order to focus on your inner core, so picture yourself as being sentenced to the naughty corner, smiling slyly, and rejoicing in the opportunity to have some time for yourself.

Think about your day, and find a time when you can have 20 minutes to yourself. Friends, colleagues and family members will continue to demand your attention, but you have to ignore their demands and assert yourself, telling them firmly that this is your time. You deserve it. Even it means doing it after everyone else has gone to sleep, or before they wake, find the time!

Meditation is really easy. There is no mystery to it. There is an apocryphal tale of an urban Englishman coming across an old country-dweller who was sitting on a bench, staring into the distance with his hands resting on his walking-stick.

"Do you come often to this place?", asked the urbanite.

"Yes, Sir", replied the countryman, "Most every day."

"And what do you do here?", the urbanite continued. The countryman replied "Well mostly I sits and thinks, but sometimes I just sits."

EXERCISE 5

First, find a comfortable position that you can maintain without fatigue for 20 minutes. You can lie, sit or stand. Personally, I prefer to sit on a fairly hard chair that has a straight back, as I tend to fall asleep if I meditate lying down. Close your eyes. Consciously relax all the muscles of your body by first tensing them and then letting them relax, starting at your toes and working upwards - feet, calves, thighs, pelvic floor, stomach, chest, hands, arms, shoulders, neck, and facial muscles. Take a deep breath via your nose, and exhale slowly from your mouth without forcing the air out, then breathe steadily and rhythmically.

The next step is to clear your mind completely, which may prove harder at first than you expect. A good way to do it is to take your full given name: picture it and speak it in your mind as you exhale. With each successive exhalation, remove the final letter until nothing remains. For example:

JOSEPH WATKINS
JOSEPH WATKIN
JOSEPH WATKI
JOSEPH WATK
JOSEPH WAT
JOSEPH WA
JOSEPH W
JOSEPH
JOSEP
JOSE
JOS
JO
J

*

Your mind is now blank, and you are thinking of nothing. Try to maintain this for as long as possible. Thoughts will, of course, start to invade your head again before long. "Did I turn the gas off? I need to buy some milk. What time is that meeting tomorrow?" etc. You can deal with this inner dialogue in a couple of ways. One method is to 'see' the thought and encase it in a bubble, then watch as it floats away beyond the periphery of your vision. Another method is to stand back from the thoughts and watch them dispassionately. Your mind likes to be active, but it does not like to be watched. Think of your mind as a dog that is released in the park to play. It will run around, sniffing at everything; just watch it, without identifying with it. Keep your distance from it, and it will eventually come to heel.

Apart from the internal distractions, there will inevitably be external distractions: someone in your household might drop a saucepan, or you hear a car horn from the street outside. Instead of getting angry at such interruptions, simply register them and let them go. You will eventually find that very little gets through to you once you are 'in the zone'.

If you find, after a few days of practice, that you are still having trouble keeping your mind blank, you can introduce some repetitive vocal phrase or tactile action to maintain stillness. For example, repeat a meaningless word such as 'doowaddle' aloud with every exhalation, or gently and repetitively press the tips of your thumbs and forefingers together.

You may find that images start to form in your inner vision, even though your eyes are closed; images which have nothing to do with your conscious thoughts. These, too, you should simply register and then release. Attach no importance to them, but do record them afterwards in your magical diary. Once you have established the habit of meditating daily, you may find it so enjoyable that you don't want to come out of it. It is therefore a good idea to set a timer alarm (most modern mobile 'phones have them) to remind you when to end the session. On ending the session, open your eyes, give yourself a minute or two to come back to normal awareness, and then write down your experiences in your magical diary.

So why meditate? After all, there is no evidence that it formed any part of a magician's training in the ancient Nordic world[11], and much evidence that it was introduced to the Western world only in the 19th Century. On the other hand, it is now a core practice in the discipline of virtually any occult organisation that you will find today. The aim of the exercise

---

11 In fact, we know virtually nothing of a magician's training in the ancient Nordic world, except by inference, so we have to filch ideas from other traditions. There is nothing wrong with that; our ancestors were also practical people who adopted a good idea when they saw it.

is to teach yourself to empty your mind of all distractions, thereby enabling you to either receive input from forces and entities outside of yourself, or to focus your mind on concepts and intentions, and to project these to the world outside. This book will focus on the latter. When performing magic, you will need to keep your mind absolutely focused on the intention, and on the forms, sounds and gestures that contribute to its accomplishment. For our ancestors in the pre-industrial age, like the old countryman in the apocryphal story I mentioned, this would have come more naturally; they had fewer distractions. These days, with the tendency to constantly attend to text messages, email and the latest news, we need to make a willed effort to achieve stillness.

Perform this exercise for seven days before moving on to the next step.

Visualisation

Once you are used to emptying your mind and ignoring distraction (whether internal or external), you can pursue a more active path in your daily exercises. As will become clear in subsequent chapters, imagination is at the heart of magical practice. Some people, especially those who like to see themselves as 'solid' and 'practical', tend to be dismissive of imagination - especially when it is mentioned in connection with magic! They interpret a capacity for imagination as being fanciful and unrealistic, and it must be admitted that many people with an interest in the occult do have such a tendency. However, consider this: there is nothing that was ever invented, no system for doing things better or for achieving results more easily, which was not first conceived in the imagination. Everything, from the first simple tools to space travel and the internet, was once only an idea in someone's head. Imagination is what defines us as human beings. To attain an outcome, you must first be able to imagine it in as much detail as possible, and this especially applies to practical magic. As children, many of us have an innate ability to daydream, i.e. to mentally drift into a story that we are telling ourselves, seeing and hearing events as if we were watching a movie. If you were - and perhaps still are - such a person, then be assured that this is a great ability. It shows that you are in touch with Narrative, the life-shaping force described in the previous chapter. On the other hand, daydreaming alone is unlikely to get you anywhere unless it is converted into positive and decisive action. Indeed, it can be detrimental if your daydreams often have negative outcomes, for this leads to pointless worrying and actual negative outcomes in your life. It is for this reason that you will need to train yourself in disciplined visualisation. Although the term 'visualisation' is derived from 'visual', i.e. pertaining to the faculty of sight, we will use it here to refer to all the natural senses, including hearing, touch, smell, and taste[12].

When training yourself to visualise, it is best to start with small, simple items and build up to bigger scenarios. This may prove harder at first than visualising more familiar, expansive situations based on everyday experience, but it is essential to achieve precision. It is also indispensable to the active use of symbolism, which we will come to later.

EXERCISE 6

After relaxing and stilling your mind, as you did in Exercise 5, picture before you a blank, dark screen as though you are in a darkened cinema before the film begins. Now picture a single point of light, like a star, in the centre of the screen. Try to hold that image for a while. You will probably find that the point tends to drift, jump about or expand; stay calm, and will the image back each time to its original form and position. Now visualise the point of light extending into a line - up, down, horizontally, or in any direction you wish. Again, hold that image for as long as you are able; if it changes, will it back into the single line that you dictate. Once

---

[12] Unfortunately, the English language (usually so diverse and multi-faceted) has no commonly used words to encompass the senses other than sight. Instead of using clumsy neologisms such as 'audibilise' or 'auralise', therefore, we will stick to 'visualise' to cover all of them.

you can hold a picture of a single line consistently, add another line at an angle to the first, and then a third line to form an equilateral triangle (that is, with all sides of equal length). Examine it: is the point at the top or at the bottom? How does this make you feel? Trying reversing its orientation. Do you feel differently about it? Devote 20 minutes daily to this exercise (including preparation by stilling your mind), and record your results in your magical diary.

EXERCISE 6a

When you can visualise a triangle consistently (always starting from a single point), move on to other 2-dimensional shapes such as a square, a pentagon (5-sided), a hexagon (6-sided) and a circle. Play with them in your mind's eye; for example, you might want to superimpose a triangle on a circle. Have fun with the shapes, and enjoy developing your ability to manipulate them. When you feel you can do this with ease, and can always visualise your desired 2-dimensional shape holding steady, move on to a 3-dimensional shape such as a cube. Rotate it before you, viewing it from all sides[13].

EXERCISE 6b

When you can perform the above two exercises proficiently, visualise a small box - a matchbox, perhaps. Imagine it holding in a steady position while you move around it, viewing it from all angles. See it also from the inside, as if you were sitting inside it. Finally, really stretch your mind and try to see it from every angle at once, including from the inside. If you can do this, then you can be confident that you really have trained your mind to visualise forms!

---

[13] If you have difficulty visualising 3-dimensional geometric forms, it may help to obtain a set of the multi-faceted dice commonly used in 'Dungeons & Dragons'. These are widely available for little expense.

Colour

You may now review your progress so far and reflect on your experiences. In what colour did you visualise those points, lines and shapes? Was it in monochrome (e.g. white lines on a black background or vice versa), or did you see them in other colours? The aspect of colour is extremely important in magic, as it connects powerfully and viscerally with our emotions. Some magical traditions dictate the associations that certain colours should hold for us, but these vary from culture to culture, and in northern magic there are few fixed associations. I therefore hold that it is better to work with the emotive associations that colours hold for you, as an individual. After all, the magic has to come from your mind, not someone else's. On a page of your magical diary, write a list of colours and describe the connections and emotions they hold for you. You might be surprised at the variations and contradictions that each may have. Here, for example, are a few of my own colour associations:

- RED: Fire; anger; blood; power; red rose; passion; sexuality; cardinal's/judge's robe; authority; holly berry; Yuletide.
- ORANGE: Autumn; rust; dust; Africa; Hallowe'en; warmth; comfort; prosperity.
- YELLOW: Sunshine; butter; noon; gold; harvest; daffodils; springtime.
- GREEN: Nature; hope; fertility; peace; copper; Ireland; Robin Hood; relaxing.
- BLUE: Sky; sea; cold; sadness; cornflowers; airmail; summer; electricity.
- WHITE: Purity; snow; surgery; death; surrender.
- BLACK: Darkness; mystery; midnight; sleep; depth.

As you can see, even this brief list has a fair variety of significances. The following exercises will help you to determine what significance each colour has for you, so that you can employ them in your magical operations.

EXERCISE 7

Relax and empty your mind, as you should be doing at the start of all your meditations (see Exercise 5). Now picture a bright, glowing cloud in a colour of your choice. Allow it to expand until it floods your vision and you are in an environment of that pure, single colour. Note the effect it has on your emotions, and the associations it arouses in your mind and memory. After completing the entire exercise, make a record of your experiences in your magical diary. Over subsequent days, repeat this with different colours, remembering to include white and black. You can also vary the shades and hues of the colours, as these may have quite different significances for you. When you have been through the entire spectrum and the various shades, start over and go through them again. Always record the results in your diary. Has anything changed? Are you perceiving the colours differently? Has one significance started to take priority over the others? Eventually you should be able to compose a list of colours and the primary significances they have for you. If you wish, you can give yourself a break and intersperse these colour-oriented exercises with others of a different nature. Discipline is important, but boredom is stultifying, so make sure you can always approach the work with excitement and enthusiasm.

EXERCISE 7a

Return to Exercise 6a, but this time visualise the geometric shapes in colours. Explore your feelings about the shape/colour combinations. How does a shape 'feel' in one colour, as opposed to another? Does it arouse different associations for you? Is there one particular colour which feels more 'right' for a certain shape than others? And what if you move a shape so that it is oriented in a different direction (for example, a triangle that points upward as opposed to one which points downward)? Record these experiences, too, in your diary. You may well find that your perceptions accord with the fixed form/colour combinations of other magical traditions. If you have already explored other traditions, you may also, consciously or unconsciously, be bringing their associations - 'correspondences' - into your own visualisation. If so, it matters not; the main thing is that you feel comfortable with the system that you are developing.

EXERCISE 7b

As well as visualisation, practise synthesizing the experiences of the other senses: hearing, scent, taste and touch.

- Think of a word, and imagine that you are hearing it spoken by someone else. Hear it spoken in a normal, conversational tone; hear it whispered; hear it shouted. Hear it in different voices, such as female and male, or a child's voice, or with different accents. You can also synthesize, in your imagination, non-vocal sounds such as thunder or a musical instrument.

- Imagine a familiar scent such as roses, onions, wine, tobacco smoke or gun oil - whatever is most evocative to you. You may wish to experiment with incenses, burning them, memorising the scent, and then recalling them in their absence.

- Experience, in its absence, the taste of something familiar; an orange, for example. Try different tastes and mentally record how they make you feel.

- Finally, explore the sense of touch in your imagination. With empty hands, feel the texture of various surfaces such as fur, tree bark, sandpaper and metal.

It is important to remember that your 20-minute daily sessions are only part of your day: the part of the day when you make a concentrated effort to enhance your magical skills. That leaves more than 23 hours per day when you are still working at them - even when you sleep! If you have never done any magical work before, you may find by now that your life, and your perception of your immediate environment, is already changing. You may feel more alert and insightful. Perhaps you may be more inclined to approach everyday events in a relaxed manner, to say less and to listen more. Your dreams may also change and apparently acquire a new significance. If so, be sure to write them down, no matter how strange they seem. The very act of writing down a dream can often lead you towards its true meaning. When out and about, be observant. Make a trip into town or a walk in the park an extension of your meditation exercises by trying to shut down the inner chatter of your mind. Observe the objects around you without naming them. When we name something, we categorise it, neatly sum up our expectations of it, and then quietly dismiss it from our consciousness. In doing so, we overlook a lot of the sheer awesomeness that surrounds us. So, instead of naming and dismissing, look at familiar objects as if you have never seen them before and have no name for them, noting their shape, motion, colour (and variations of colour), texture, odour, and sound. Examine them in minute detail, and you may well rediscover a marvellous world that you had forgotten. If you have the leisure to do so, take up sketching; this will help you to observe such details. You don't have to be good at it: it is the attempt that counts. Soon you will begin to rediscover the thrilling sense of wonder which you experienced as a child and which was experienced by our ancestors, both human and divine.

Lastly, do not forget physical fitness. Mental faculties tend to be sharper when housed in a healthy body, so make sure to stretch your physical abilities as well as your mental abilities.

CHAPTER 3

AN INTRODUCTION TO RUNE-LORE

Now that you have begun to reawaken the god-like abilities which have lain latent in you for so long, it is time to give you some of the tools, as Rig gave to Jarl in the mythic history. It makes good sense to provide an introduction to the runes as a foundation on which to build. It will be no more than an introduction, as there are already plenty of books on the subject, and you can find a selection of these in the bibliography.

What is a rune? Many people think of them as an ancient type of writing, or characters carved on stones or tablets of wood. This is not entirely wrong, but these are only commonly encountered manifestations. In essence a rune is a mystery or secret, an essential truth of existence embodied in a four-fold expression. It is four-fold because it has the following aspects:

1) Form - the *shape* of the rune, as visualised, carved or written;
2) Phoneme - the *sound* of the rune, as uttered;
3) Number - the rune's number in the Futhark sequence;
4) The esoteric (inner) meaning of the rune.

All of these must be memorised, internalised and mastered in order to effectively use rune magic, but let us first take a look at the origins and development of the runes.

'Futhark' is a term we use to describe the row of carved or written characters that were used by Germanic peoples from antiquity. It is based on the first six characters of the row, much as 'alphabet' is derived from the first two characters of the Greek alphabet, alpha and beta. Nobody knows precisely when the Germanic peoples began to adopt the use of such characters, but the earliest known inscriptions date from the 2nd Century of the Current Era (CE). Some of the Futhark runes are apparently derived from letters of the Greek and Roman alphabets, but others are to be found nowhere else. It is most probable that indigenous symbols were mixed with characters taken from those Mediterranean sources; after all, the amount of trade and cultural mingling in the ancient world should not be underestimated. What is certain is that the Futhark row has a quite different sequence to that of the Graeco-Roman alphabet, and the Rune Poems indicate that its constituent characters have names and esoteric meanings, unlike the purely functional Roman alphabet.

As regards the inner meaning of the word as 'mystery' or 'secret', the runes already existed in undifferentiated form in the magically charged void of Ginnungagap, before time began. As already recounted in the Introduction, the discovery of the runes by Odin was the result of his sacrifice of self to self on the World-tree, Yggdrasil. It is important not to conflate the runes in their entirety with those of the Futhark-row; there are many mysteries, and nowhere in the Hávamál (Lay of the High One) is it stated that the Futhark runes were the only ones that were learned by Odin. Nevertheless, these are the ones that have been handed down to mankind, and a rich source of wisdom they are.

Although there was never any one, standardised rune-row (which can make runology a perplexing subject at times), and there are many variations in the way the characters were carved, the sequence of characters tended on the whole to remain the same. Broadly speaking, the rune-rows tend to fall into 4 main categories and periods:

- **The Elder Futhark** (c. 200-700 CE), a Proto-Germanic row of 24 characters which has no known poem associated with it. The names of the individual runes are therefore conjectural and reconstructed;
- **The Anglo-Frisian Futhorc** (c. 700-1000 CE), which was initially very similar to the Elder Futhark but was gradually extended to include up to 12 new characters and sounds. The phonetic value of some of the later characters is unknown;
- **The Younger Futhark** (c. 700-1300 CE), a Scandinavian development of the Elder Futhark which contracted the row from 24 to 16 characters. The loss of 8 characters meant that many had to 'double up' in phonetic value, such as *k/g*, *t/d* and *b/p*. Some of the esoteric lore may also have been merged or lost in the process;
- **A Mediaeval and Early Modern expansion of the Younger Futhark** in an attempt to gain better parity with the Roman alphabet. This was achieved using a system of points or dots: for example, an 'I' with a point in its centre represented the 'e' sound; a 'T' with a point represented the 'd' sound. There was also a tendency for the characters to be written (as opposed to carved) in a more cursive style instead of the angular forms better suited for carving on wood or stone. This row appears to have been mainly used as a system of writing, although there are some indications that ancient lore may have been preserved in a system of glosses or 'kennings'. Although the use of the Viking-age runes as a form of writing had seriously declined by the beginning of the early modern period, we know that they were still used in some of the Icelandic grimoires after 1500 CE. Furthermore, while it cannot be confirmed that the galdrastafir (magical staves) of the Early Modern period are in any way based on the runes, neither can this be categorically denied. We will return to this matter in more detail later.

The full rows are shown in Appendix 2, and Appendix 3 provides a discussion of the kennings.

The descriptions below cover only the 24 runes contained in the Elder Futhark, with reference to the Old English Rune Poem (OERP), the Old Norse Rune Rhyme (ONRR) and the Old Icelandic Rune Poem (OIRP). The first name given is always the conjectural Proto-Germanic name, as these names are the most commonly used among present-day runers (rune magicians). The translations of the Rune Poems into modern English are mainly derived from "Rune-Song" by Edred Thorsson, with the occasional variation of my own. The interpretations are entirely my own, and learners are encouraged to read the other sources listed in the bibliography and to explore the runes in their own meditational exercises. For the reader's convenience, I append a simple *galdor* or mantra for each rune, to be used in the exercises described in the next chapter. Alternative forms of galdor can be found in "Futhark: A Handbook of Rune Magic" by Edred Thorsson (see bibliography).

1. ᚠ FEHU / FEOH / FÉ

OERP
Feoh (Wealth) is a comfort to every man
although every man ought to deal it out freely
if he wants, before the lord, his lot of judgement.
ONRR
Fé (Gold) causes strife among kinsmen;
the wolf grows up in the woods.
OIRP
Fé (Gold) is the strife of kinsmen and the fire of the flood-tide
and the path of the serpent.

To understand this rune, we have to remember that its original meaning was 'cattle', 'sheep' or 'livestock'. Livestock was the earliest form of mobile wealth. Even today, 'fé' in Modern Icelandic can mean either 'livestock' or 'money', and our Modern English word 'fee' is derived from the same root. Similarly, our word 'pecuniary' (relating to money) is derived from the Latin cognate *pecu*, which also meant 'livestock'. Mobile wealth, unlike ancestral land, could be moved around for payment and barter. For this purpose, cattle came to be replaced by more convenient coinage in precious metals, primarily gold and silver. Over the past two centuries, the precious metals have been replaced by base metal coins, and paper IOUs issued by national banks. More recently still, even these tokens with no integral value have been replaced by purely digital transactions. Wealth and money are concepts; their outer forms are relatively unimportant. What matters is what you can do or buy with that wealth. Money may not necessarily make you happy, but it is certainly empowering. And, whether manifested as a herd of cattle or a stream of digits, that is what Fehu is about: power in its purest form. At the arcane level, it is raw, magical power, which is why this is the first rune that you should focus on and take unto yourself. The possession of it will bring power to all your workings.

The dark side of Fehu, expressed in the Rune Poems, is that it can lead to greed and envy when imbalanced. The 'wolf' mentioned in the ONRR is the dark sentiment of rapacity, which can grow in the hidden places of our hearts until it comes to control us. For that reason, one should 'deal it out freely' (i.e. be generous) unless we want to become like the dragon Fafnir jealously guarding his hoard. When balanced, Fehu is a bright, expansive rune associated with the fiery world of Muspelsheim.

Form: ᚠ, ᚡ
Phoneme: f
Number: 1
Esoteric meaning: livestock, mobile wealth, raw power
Galdor: ffffffffffffffff

2. ᚢ URUZ / ŪR / ÚR

OERP
Ūr (Aurochs) is fearless and greatly horned.
A very fierce beast, it fights with its horns.
A famous roamer of the moor, it is a courageous animal.
ONRR
Úr (Slag) is from bad iron;
oft runs the reindeer on the hard snow.
OIRP
Úr (Drizzle) is the weeping of the clouds and the diminisher of the rim of ice,
and (an object for) the herdsman's hate.

We are faced with five distinct images in these rune poems. Firstly, there is the aurochs, an extinct species of wild ox which roamed the moors and woodlands of northern Europe until Early Modern times. The last of its kind died in Poland in 1627. This huge beast - up to 160 cm or more than 5 feet tall at the shoulder - was well known to the Germanic tribes of the Migration Era. They were renowned for their fierceness and untameability, and killing one was a test of manhood. The second image is of slag coming from 'bad iron'. In Early Mediaeval northern Europe, iron was a desirable resource, but there were few places where it could be mined. Our ancestors therefore sought out 'bog iron': naturally occurring nodules of iron ore which formed in the anaerobic conditions of the plentiful bogs. The nodules were broken up and placed, together with charcoal, in primitive ovens known as 'bloomeries'. When the correct heat was attained, the iron would separate from the impurities to form a 'bloom', which could then be hammered into a purer form of iron. The impurities ran off to form unusable slag, and the more impurities there were in the ore, the greater the amount of slag. The third image is of a reindeer running on hard snow. Soft snow will, of course, impede progress: you may have had the experience of walking through knee-deep snow and know how exhausting this can be. If, however, there has been a slight thaw and a subsequent freeze, a crust can form over it, strong enough to bear man or beast. The fourth image is of drizzle falling from the sky. Again, experience will tell you that snow and ice are often reduced faster by rain than by any amount of sunshine. Is it something hateful, for the herdsman or shepherd? Well, few of us like being subjected to an unrelenting drizzle, but I would suggest that a fifth image is actually present here, unrelated to the first stanza of the OIRP. Rain is inevitable; it is part of the existence of anyone who works outdoors, and there is no point in kicking against it. What the shepherd hates most is the tup who is wilful, who constantly wanders and will not stay with the flock. It takes time and effort to bring him back and, in the meantime, he has to neglect the main flock.

The main concept to be drawn from these five, apparently disparate images is one of wildness and uncontrollability. The aurochs were wild and could not be domesticated; impurities in iron ore made the outcome uncertain; a reindeer might get away from its herder when able to run freely on a sound surface; drizzle will quickly bring down the structures wrought by ice; and, like the reindeer running away, the sheep that will not follow the flock is the object of the shepherd's hate.

In mythology, the cosmic cow Auðumla fed Ymir with her milk, but she also licked away the block of salty ice that held Búri, the grandfather of Odin, Vili and Vé. Those three brothers were destined to bring down the established order of the Giants and impose a new order based on their own concepts. Auðumla was the catalyst in this process.

Uruz is diametrically opposed to concepts of order and structure. It is the rune of rebellion, and a force which can bring down established structures and modes of behaviour. It can be used to break existing patterns, but should be used with care. In mediaeval Iceland, ice bridges facilitated travel and communication when rivers froze, and their destruction (come the thaw and with rain) recreated a hindrance. Uruz is the rune of the anarchist, the Bohemian and the libertarian, but like all the runes it must be used wisely.

Form: ᚢ, ᚤ
Phoneme: u (pronounced 'oo')
Number: 2
Esoteric meaning: wildness; refusal to obey; breaking of strictures and established structure.
Galdor: uuuuuuuuuuuuuu

3. ᚦ THURISAZ / ÞORN / ÞURS

OERP
þorn (Thorn) is very sharp; for every thegn
who grasps it, it is harmful, and exceedingly cruel
to every man who lies upon it.
ONRR
þurs (Thurs) causes the sickness of women;
few are cheerful from misfortune.
OIRP
þurs (Thurs) is the torment of women and the dweller in the rocks
and the husband of 'varðrúna'.

Little good can be said of this rune, to judge from the Rune Poems. It is the embodiment of discomfort, misfortune, and sickness - especially, for some reason, for women. Its name in the OERP is 'Thorn', which means exactly what it does in Modern English. In the ONNR and the OIRP, it is called 'Thurs'. A Thurs, in Nordic mythology, is a giant of an especially brutish and savage kind, bent on the destruction of the gods and all their works, including humankind.

It would at first appear that this rune is good only for cursing and other acts of malevolent magic - for which it is indeed useful. However, the 'Thorn' aspect is also extremely useful for acts of warding or protection, or for getting rid of unwanted guests. Every night, before going to bed, it is good to ward one's home by projecting the image of a dense hedge of thorns around it, especially at the main entrances. Guests who outstay their welcome can be induced to leave by projecting the thorn-rune onto the place where they usually sit or lie; they will not be able to settle comfortably, and will soon depart.

Many modern magicians in the Northern Tradition also think of this as the rune of Ása-Þórr, 'Thor of the Gods'. The son of Odin and his first consort, Jorð (Earth), Thor is the gods' answer to the destructive power of the Thurses. Immensely strong, armed with a mighty hammer which always returns to his hand after throwing, this storm-god takes the view that offence is the best form of defence and goes out to kill as many giants as he can in order to protect Asgard and Midgard. He has no time for niceties or subtle negotiation.

Based upon my own insights and experiences, I think of Thurisaz as the 'smash and grab' rune: powerfully directed force that can smash a way through when all else has failed, or when you don't have the time or inclination for subtlety. It also gives mighty protection against harm (cf. Elhaz below).

Form: ᚦ, Þ
Phoneme: th, as in 'thorn', 'think' or 'thrust'
Number: 3
Esoteric meaning: Thorn; giant; Thor (and his hammer); violent force; discomfort; protection
Galdor: thththththththththth or thu tha thi the tho

4. ᚨ ANSUZ / ŌS / ÓSS / ÁSS

OERP
Ōs (God) is the chieftain of all speech,
the mainstay of wisdom and comfort to the wise,
for every noble warrior help and happiness.
ONRR
Óss (A god) is the way of most journeys,
but the sheath is (that way for) swords.
OIRP

Áss (A god) is the olden-father and Asgard's chieftain and the leader of Valhalla.

Ansuz is the rune *par excellence* of Odin (also known as Óðinn, Woden, or Wotan), chief among the Aesir, the elder gods of the Germanic peoples. Master of magic, speech, poetry, writing and inspiration, Odin is a cunning god who travels widely in his never-ending quest for wisdom. Unlike Thor, subtlety and trickery are second nature to him, and he is often prepared to seek out the company of Etins (another race of giants) if he thinks he can learn something from them. He also has a dark side as a god of war and a necromancer (i.e. one who is able to call upon the dead for information), and extensive blood-offerings - including human sacrifice - were made to him in olden days. Woden is also the Lord of the Wild Hunt, the sudden, raging gale that can pass in the autumn and winter months. He rescued the Mead of Inspiration from the Etins, and cast one of his eyes into Mimir's Well, where it sees all things, past, present and future.

Ansuz is always a good rune to use when inspiration is needed for deeds connected with speech, writing or poetry, or when the rede (counsel) of the Aesir is required. Focusing on the rune and chanting it for several minutes before settling down to writing can raise your wōd, allowing you to compose prose or poetry in a divinely inspired state. It helps also to call upon this rune before acts of divination or operative magic.

- Form: ᚨ (Note that this is the Elder Futhark form; for variants, see Appendix 2)
- Phoneme: ā, as in 'father' (again, the value can differ, becoming 'o' as in 'god')
- Number: 4
- Esoteric meaning: Ancestral god; Odin; divinely-sourced inspiration; divine counsel; knowledge
- Galdor: aaaaaaaaaaaaaaaa

5. ᚱ RAIÐO / RĀD / REIÐ

OERP
Rād (Riding) is, in the hall, to every warrior
easy, but very hard for the one who sits up
on a powerful horse over miles of road.

ONRR
Reið (Riding), it is said, is the worst for horses;
Reginn forged the best sword.

OIRP
Reið (Riding) is a blessed sitting and a swift journey
and the toil of the horse.

In all three of the poems, this rune is unequivocally connected with riding a horse. There are differences in emphasis; the OERP appears to speak of the strain imposed on the rider, rather than the horse, saying that it is easy to speak of riding when sitting comfortably indoors, but the actual deed is harder. In the modern idiom, "You can talk the talk, but can you walk the walk?" The message of the ONRR and the OIRP is different, emphasising the toil of the horse as opposed to the ease of the rider, and saying, in effect, "Let the horse take the strain."

Overall, this rune is about travel, journeys, and everything connected, as evidenced by the Latin gloss 'iter' (journey) to the Icelandic poem. The Modern English word 'road' is derived from the same root. There may also be a connection with the German word 'Rad' (wheel). Although this is not supported by the Rune Poems, it must be remembered that horses were first used as draught animals to pull wheeled conveyances, from farm carts to war chariots. Association with the wheel opens up many other concepts of a circular and iterative nature, such as ritual, recurrence, routine (itself derived from the French word for 'road') and the daily and annual cycles of the sun, moon and other heavenly bodies.

Raiðo has many applications in rune-magic. It can be evoked for any operation connected with travel; for example (in combination with Elhaz), to have a safe journey. It can also be used to help establish beneficial routines or to learn rituals, so that you can perform them with a minimum of conscious thought and free your mind to focus on the attainment of the aim. A useful example here is driving a car: most of us can remember how clumsy we were at the beginning, how every move had to be consciously planned and thought about. With practice, however, it becomes a learned habit, so that we can perform this ritual unconsciously and safely arrive at our destination with minimum effort. In tandem with other runes, Raiðo also governs lunar and seasonal rituals, these being connected with monthly and annual journeys of the moon and sun.

The second stanza of the Old Norwegian Rune Rhyme, "Reginn forged the best sword" is somewhat baffling until one remembers that the smith's work also involves a great number of ritualistic, repetitive operations which the smith must learn and practice until they become second nature. Raiðo is about doing things right, and in the right order.

Form: R
Phoneme: a trilled 'r'
Number: 5
Esoteric meaning: Riding; travel; journeys; repetitive action; cycles; routine
Galdor: a trilled 'rrrrrrrrrrrr'

6. KENAZ / CEN / KAUN

OERP
Cen (Torch) is to every living person known by its fire
it is clear and bright; it usually burns
when the noblemen rest inside the hall.
ONRR
Kaun (Sore) is the curse of children;
grief makes a man pale.

OIRP
Kaun (Sore) is the bale of children and a scourge[14]
and the house of rotten flesh.

In Kenaz, the Rune Poems present us with two apparently irreconcilable images. In the OERP, we have the image of a torch burning clearly and brightly in the hall. In the ONRR and the OIRP, on the other hand, we have images of sores, ulcers, scars, and grief. It is not known why such a contrast should exist, and many runers simply give up trying to reconcile them, focusing only on the more optimistic stanzas of the OERP. I suggest that these contrasting concepts once formed a single, paradoxical concept in an early stage of rune-lore, but the bright and dark sides became detached from each other. Similar paradoxes can be seen in the case of other runes such as Fehu, which encompasses the benefits of wealth, and the dangers inherent in greed and envy.

The 'Cen' (Torch) of the OERP is in any case about a flame; a controlled fire which illuminates its surroundings and penetrates darkness. It usually burns when the *aethelingas*, or noblemen, rest inside the hall. In esoteric terms, this may represent the most noble among humankind resting in a meditative state. Kenaz may also be etymologically connected to *ken-*, the root of 'know', 'knowledge', 'cunning' and 'can' (be able) in most Germanic languages. Knowledge, like the torch, penetrates the darkness. Herein could lie the meaning of the murky flip-side embodied in the Norwegian and Icelandic poems, for flame can burn and scour the flesh, and knowledge can be a dangerous thing if imperfectly understood and applied. To gain knowledge and ability, one must be prepared to experiment and sometimes incur scars. The burnt child fears the flame.

Form: ᚲ (Elder Futhark), ᚳ (Anglo-Frisian Futhorc), or ᚴ (Younger Futhark)

---

14 Or perhaps 'scar'.

Phoneme: k
Number: 6
Esoteric meaning: Torch; light; knowledge; ability; cunning; the scars and grief incurred in the pursuit of knowledge.
Galdor: k - k - k - k - k *or* ku ka ki ke ko

7. ᚷ GEBO / GYFU

OERP
Gyfu (Gift) is for every man a pride and praise,
help and worthiness; (and) of every homeless adventurer,
it is estate and substance for those who have nothing else.
(The rune is not present in the ONRR and OIRP.)

The G-rune is all about gifts, giving, exchange and rewards. Giving was an important matter in Early Mediaeval Germanic society, and remains so to this day. The mutual exchange of gifts cemented bonds of friendship and alliance, and helped to heal past enmities. Warrior nobles were expected to be generous to their followers (often 'homeless adventurers' among the Viking armies), and failure to give due reward would lead to loss of loyalty. Hospitality, too, was important in a society consisting of scattered settlements connected only by poor roads and tracks. One never knew when one might be in need of food and shelter from a stranger if benighted along the road. At the same time, there had to be reciprocity: in exchange for his Lord's generosity, a warrior was expected to abide by his oaths and be loyal unto death; hospitality, though expected, was not to be abused by outstaying the welcome. It was also crucial not to create an imbalance, for a gift engenders a debt on the part of the recipient; by giving too much - more than the recipient was able to give in return - one might create resentment. Many examples of the ancient attitude towards giving are to be found in the Eddas (particularly in the Hávamál) and in the sagas. My favourite is verse 44 of the Hávamál:

> *"If you know that you have a friend, and that he is true,*
> *and that you will get good from him,*
> *share your mind with him, exchange gifts,*
> *and visit him often."*

In fact, little has changed to this day in that respect. An employer who underpays his staff and offers no fringe benefits cannot expect to retain their loyalty. Business relationships are improved by the exchange of small gifts, and more by the willingness to 'go the extra mile' for a customer or supplier when times get hard. The prime time for giving today is Yuletide; who has not had the experience of feeling embarrassed or disgruntled when the gifts are imbalanced? In the end, the greatest gift one can give or receive is unstinting friendship, but that will ultimately break down if it becomes one-sided. Balance is all.

Form: X
Phoneme: hard 'g' as in 'gift'
Number: 7
Esoteric meaning: Gift; giving; reward; exchange; mutuality; balance
Galdor: g - g - g - g - g *or* gu ga gi ge go

8. ᚹ WUNJO / WYN

OERP
Wyn (Joy) is had by the one who knows few troubles,
pains or sorrows, and to him who himself has
power and blessedness, and also the plenty of towns[15].
(The rune is not present in the ONRR and OIRP.)

The lines in the OERP seem to state the obvious: joy is to be had in the absence of troubles, pains or sorrows, especially when you have 'power and blessedness' and the plenty that is to be had in civilised communities. And who would disagree with that? Most of us, even at a comparatively early age, have

---

15 A better translation is 'fortified enclosure' or 'burgh'.

known - or think we have known - some adversity, and would not regret its absence. At first sight, there appears to be no rune (mystery) here, only a bland platitude. The key lies in relativity, and the Anglo-Saxons were fully familiar with that concept, as evidenced by the Old English poem 'The Wanderer' describing the sadness of a man as he reflects on joys past and his present miserable condition. To take but one verse of this poem:

> *"All is troublesome in this earthy kingdom;*
> *the turn of events changes the world under the heavens.*
> *Here money is fleeting, here friend is fleeting,*
> *Here man is fleeting, here kinsman is fleeting;*
> *All the foundation of this world turns to waste!"*

Joy and misery are but two sides of the same coin. You cannot appreciate the one without having experienced the other. Those who constantly shun adversity will never know true joy. The real warrior-of-life, on the other hand, will seek out adversity to test his mettle, in the knowledge that it will better enable him to savour real happiness. Riches and security do not automatically lead to joy. Indeed, they can frequently lead to a sense of emptiness and restlessness that many, in our modern society, seek to fill with acquisition of even more pointless possessions. Nobody is better equipped to savour a warm, sheeted bed, a full belly, and a secure home than the soldier who has too often slept in a wet trench, on half rations, accompanied by the imminent threat of death. In the end, this rune is about the harmony of mind which comes when you have known both ends of the spectrum and gained confidence in your ability to endure, whatever the future brings. The rune can be used for any working to improve happiness and harmony.

Form: ᚹ
Phoneme: w, as in 'wonder'
Number: 8
Esoteric meaning: Joy; harmony; contentment; equanimity

Galdor: wwwwwwwww (somewhat difficult) or wun wan win wen won

Thus ends the first *ætt* (family) of the Futhark, for the 24-rune row is divided into three *ættir*, each of 8 runes. (æ is pronounced as the English word 'eye'.)

9. ᚺ HAGALAZ / HAEGL / HAGALL

OERP

Haegl (Hail) is the whitest of grains; it comes from high in heaven.
A shower of wind hurls it, then it turns to water.

ONRR

Hagall (Hail) is the coldest of grains;
Christ shaped the world in ancient times.

OIRP

Hagall (Hail) is a cold grain and a shower of sleet
and the sickness of snakes.

The import of this rune is unequivocal in all three poems: it represents hail or sleet. Given the snowflake form of the rune in the Younger Futhark (✳), it could also represent snow. In any case, it stands for icy precipitation from the heavens. Falls of hail are common enough, but when hail falls heavily it can inflict substantial damage. Unlike snow and sleet, hail falls most often in summer, being generated in the atmospheric convection currents which also generate thunderstorms. Coming from the sky without warning, it can beat down standing crops; very big hailstones can also inflict injury on man and beast, or even cause damage to buildings. Once fallen, it melts, providing water for the same crops that it has beaten down, and the crops often recover after a day or two. As a sudden fall of ice in the summer, when snakes are active, it would be harmful for these cold-blooded creatures, slowing them down and making them easier prey.

The second line of the ONRR, "Christ shaped the world in ancient times", may have originally read "Hroptr (a byname of Odin) shaped the world in ancient times." This line, together with the position of Hagalaz as the ninth rune in the row, gives a clue to its role as a structural foundation for all of creation. Edred Thorsson makes much of this aspect of Hagalaz in its snowflake form, referring to it as the 'mother rune' when enclosed in a hexagon; within this glyph, all the other rune-forms may be found. Personally, I found that I could not unite with Edred's great emphasis on this wholly benign aspect of the rune. When I first devoted my focused attention to it in a series of meditations and exercises over a week, I was met with a series of minor disasters. I realised in time that I had to confront the rune again and, being wary, I consulted other interpretations. Freya Aswynn, in her book "Leaves of Yggdrasil", admits of the rune's dangerous aspects but also connects it with the Germanic goddess (or perhaps Norn) Frau Holle, who is the matron of spinning, industriousness, good housekeeping and kindliness. While I was performing a series of daily devotional exercises to Frau Holle, I saw a large field of grass on a sunny September afternoon, apparently covered in shining frost. The 'frost', however was moving and undulating in the breeze! On closer inspection, it turned out to be covered in millions of gossamer threads from baby spiders - nature's spinners. In the same week, my daughter asked if I would volunteer to accompany a school trip. "Sure", I replied", where will we be going?" "The Bradford Museum of Spinning and Weaving", she said. I knew then that I was on the right track. Frau Holle is a goddess who will try you at first, but if you have the qualities that she prizes, she will give great rewards. I encountered no setbacks during this second approach to the rune, and came out with a feeling of wholeness that was in tune with the snowflake form as perceived by Edred Thorsson.

Hagalaz is therefore a rune best approached with caution. It has two distinct forms, and to get to the one you must first overcome the other. In its Elder Futhark form (ᚺ) it represents a crisis that will bring progress if handled correctly. Two uprights are connected by a bar that slopes downward, indicating that you must sometimes fall in order to move forward. It can be an unpleasant but necessary process. Do it right, digest the lessons, and you will be rewarded by the wholeness of the snowflake form.

Hagalaz in its Elder Futhark form is often used to put a curse on enemies. I do not generally approve of curses and - *if* I were to use it in this way - I would frame it as a blessing so that a particularly nasty person had the opportunity to reflect on their Wyrd and improve themself. The snowflake form can be used to hallow a stead before a magical working for maximum magical effect - but be sure that you have made this rune your own first!

Form: Elder Futhark ᚺ; Anglo-Frisian Futhorc ᚺ; Younger Futhark ᚼ

Phoneme: h, as in 'hail'

Number: 9

Esoteric meaning: Hail; a sudden disaster which ultimately brings good; wholeness; framework on which to build

Galdor: a voiceless hhhhhhhhhh

10. ᚾ NAUÐIZ / NȲD / NAUÐ

OERP
Nȳd (Need) is constricting on the chest
although to the children of men it often becomes
a help and a salvation nevertheless
if they heed it in time.

ONRR
Nauð (Need) makes for a difficult situation;
the naked freeze in the frost.

OIRP
Nauð (Need) is the grief of the bondmaid and a hard condition
and toilsome work.

Nauðiz (Need) describes the restrictions and impediments that one may encounter in life, whether for lack of money (see Fehu) or because of other factors that present us with difficulties. No matter how well we plan, all too often our plans go awry due to unforeseen circumstances. When much is at stake, and when many hindrances come at once, an anxiety may be created which makes it hard to breathe. The latter response is, however, not at all helpful and, in such situations, it is far better to take deep breaths, calm down, and consider how you can overcome the obstacles. The rune is about friction; its very form resembles two crossed rods rubbing together to kindle a 'need-fire', which would be a very sensible idea if you should find yourself freezing in the frost. Necessity is the mother of invention, and most human inventions and natural adaptations come only in response to need. Friction is, in fact, a vital factor in progress of any kind. Too often these days, we are told that the trains cannot run because of snow or ice on the tracks: then there is no friction, and the wheels (see Raiðo above, and Isa below) of the train spin uselessly. Nauðiz is the rune which enables us to manifest ideas on the physical plane, and it is probably synchronous that the Magician in the Rider-Waite Tarot pack adopts a posture resembling the Need-rune.

THE MAGICIAN CARD FROM THE RIDER-WAITE TAROT PACK

This rune can therefore be used in operations designed to overcome impediments by means of inventiveness.

Form: ᚾ

Phoneme: n

Number: 10

Esoteric meaning: Need; impedance; friction; kindling; inventiveness in response to adversity

Galdor: nnnnnnnnnnn

11. ᛁ ISA / ĪS / ÍS

(note that the 'i' is pronounced 'ee' and the 's' is sibilant, as in 'snake')

OERP

Īs (Ice) is very cold and exceedingly slippery;
it glistens, clear as glass, very much like gems;
a floor made of frost is fair to see.

ONRR

Ís (Ice) we call the broad bridge;
the blind need to be led.

OIRP

Ís (Ice) is the rind of the river and the roof of the waves
and a danger for fey[16] men.

Ice is, of course, very familiar to the inhabitants of the cold reaches of northern Europe. Beautiful to look at, it holds perils but also brings benefits. Though there is always the danger of slipping and falling, ice can also create a path. In Iceland, even until the beginning of the 20th Century, there were few bridges to span the many rivers. In summer it might require a detour of many miles to find a fordable spot, but in winter the rivers often freeze over and can then be crossed on foot or on horseback. At the coast, it can form pack-ice on the sea (the roof of the waves) in a harsh winter, trapping and perhaps

---

16 Fey = doomed to die.

crushing the boat of anyone unfortunate enough to sail into such conditions.

Above all, though, the chilling cold of ice brings stillness. Growth ceases and almost all life comes to a halt. In Nordic mythology, ice was one of the two forces (the other being fire) which initiated the entire process of creation. Esoterically, Isa represents the force of contraction and hardening. That which was fluid, and therefore less predictable, becomes solid and static. Too much of it will kill you, but in the right amount, and at the right place, it can form a bridge across an otherwise impassable barrier. The form of the rune should, perhaps, actually be a point, representing everything contracting into nothingness, but as that would be impossible to see we can consider it as a point extended into a line, rather as the ice of Niflheim extended into Ginnungagap to meet the fire emanating from Muspelsheim.

For magical purposes, you can use Isa to slow things down and impose calm when situations become dangerously fluid and threaten to overwhelm you. It is also an excellent rune to meditate on, at any time, to gain stillness. If you are using the runes as a system of divination, it can indicate that now is not the time for action; use your time instead to make plans and solidify your thoughts.

Form: |
Phoneme: a long 'i' as in English 'ee'
Number: 11
Esoteric meaning: Ice; cold; contraction; stillness; solidifying force
Galdor: iiiiiiiiiiiiiii (sounds like English 'eeeeee')

12. JERA / ĠĒR / ÁR

OERP
Ġēr (Harvest) is the hope of men, when god lets,
holy king of heaven, the earth give her bright fruits
to the nobles and needy.
ONRR

Ár (Harvest) is the profit of men;
I say that Fróði was generous.
OIRP
Ár (Harvest) is the profit of all men, and a good summer, and a ripened field.

Jera is the cyclical mystery of the passing seasons of the year, with emphasis on the 'good' season of growth and harvest. It comes after the cycle of three runes representing ice, hail, snow, and hardship. Icelandic kennings outside of the Rune Poem also refer to hay fields, luxuriant meadows, bird song, and travel by ship or boat. 'Fróði' is a reference to the god Frey, who presides over the fertility of crops, beasts and men. It is the comfortable time of year, free of frost, when crops can be grown and harvested, when livestock fattens and bears young, and when vessels can venture out safely to gather the harvest of the seas. In harvest lies hope, for people living on the edge in a subsistence economy. A good harvest may guarantee survival through the winter; a poor one famine, hardship and death. This is a rune of 'what goes around, comes around'. The harvest that you reap will depend on how well you sow and tend your crops. In a wider sense, the rune refers to the benefit of good and wise conduct throughout one's life, in one's dealings with one's fellow men and in the handling of the cards that life deals. In the broadest sense of all, this is the rune of the cyclical nature of the year and the sun, ever arising, becoming, declining, dying, and arising again. As number 12 in the 24-rune row of the Elder Futhark, it occupies the centre place together with Eihwaz (number 13), and I like to see it as the physical plane, ever revolving around the vertical axis of consciousness that is represented by Eihwaz. In magical operations, the rune can be used to bring a fruitful conclusion to one's efforts.

>Form: Elder Futhark ᛃ; Younger Futhark ᛆ
>Phoneme: 'y' as in 'year', or for Younger Futhark an Icelandic 'á', pronounced similarly to English 'ow' as in 'powder'

Number: 12

Esoteric meaning: Year; harvest; summer; due reward (based on past action)

Galdor: yu ya yi ye yo *or* ooooo -try to say an extended 'ow', but never reaching the point at which you bring your lips together for the 'w'.

13. ᛇ EIHWAZ / ĒOH / ÝR

OERP
Ēoh (Yew) is on the outside a rough tree
and hard, firm in the earth, keeper of the fire;
supported by roots, (it is a) joy on the estate.
ONRR
Ýr (Yew) is the greenest wood in winter;
there is usually, when it burns, singeing.
OIRP
Ýr (Yew) is a strong bow, and a tool of battle,
and a giant of the arrow.

The Yew-rune is something of an enigma in the rune rows. In the Elder Futhark and the Anglo-Frisian Futhorc, it holds 13th place, and is therefore central (together with Jera), but in the Younger Futhark it holds the final, sixteenth place. Furthermore, the form differs, being ᛇ in the elder rows and ᛦ in the younger row. In the latter, its name is Ýr and its phonetic value is the final -R which terminates many Old Norse words and which replaced the -Z finial of Proto-Germanic. The precise phonetic value of ᛇ is, however, unknown, and many different proposals have been made by linguistic experts[17]. Most esoteric runers today attribute to it the value of either EI, as in the German word 'Eich', or IH. Personally, I prefer the former. What is certain is that all three Rune Poems refer to the European yew tree (Taxus Baccata).

---

17 See Bernard Mees "The Yew Rune, Yogh and Yew", Leeds Studies in English, New Series XLII, University of Leeds 2011.

A stately, dark, saturnine evergreen, the yew is slow-growing and can achieve exceptional longevity, exceeding even that of the oak. In England, it is frequently found in ancient churchyards, some of which may be located on the sites of older, pre-Christian places of worship. When used as firewood, it burns slowly and produces intense heat, but it was mainly prized as a source of excellent wood for bows. As such, it is connected with the Norse archer-god Ullr, who dwells in Ýdalir (Yew Dales). It has also been suggested that the World-tree Yggdrasil may be represented as a yew rather than an ash, and this would make sense in view of the yew's evergreen nature. A feature oddly not mentioned in the Rune Poems is that all parts of the yew tree - wood, leaves, and berries - are extremely poisonous and can cause death if ingested.

The picture which emerges is of a tall, stately tree which is both stalwart and flexible, and which represents both life (in its longevity) and death (in its toxicity). The ideogram in the Elder Futhark suggests a single axis connecting the heavens and the underworld, while the Younger Futhark ideogram suggests roots reaching deep into the earth. As such, I identify this rune with the vertical axis of Yggdrasil, the long-suffering World-tree, and with steadfastness. This is the axis of consciousness, from the highest spirituality to the low-level consciousness of the autonomic nervous system. It is a good rune to invoke when one is taxed by outside circumstances, providing 'backbone', on the one hand, and flexibility on the other. It is also good for enhancing integration of all one's personal levels, from elevated, spiritual ideals down to the baser fears, desires and instincts.

> Form: ᛇ (Elder Futhark), ᛦ (Younger Futhark)
> Phoneme: 'ei', as in German 'Eich'
> Number: 13
> Esoteric meaning: The bole of Yggdrasil, connection between the heavens and the underworld, life-death-resurrection, steadfastness, flexibility.

Galdor: a long, open-throated eeeeiiiiii, as if singing the German word 'Eich' but omitting the terminal 'ch'.

14. ᛈ PERTHRO / PEORTH

OERP
Peorð (Lot-box?) is always play and laughter
among bold men, where the warriors sit
in the beer-hall, happy together.
(Not present in the ONRR or OIRP.)

If Eihwaz is an enigma, then Perthro is an almost unsolvable riddle. It occurs only in the OERP, and is absent from the ONRR and OIRP. Furthermore, the word 'Peorð' occurs only in the Rune Poem, and is not a standard word in Old English. The meaning can therefore only be inferred from the context. Many meanings have been suggested, such as gaming-board, dice-cup or lyre, for all of these could provide play and laughter in the beer hall. Regrettably, none of them provide an esoteric interpretation that can enjoy sound academic backing. Nevertheless, a choice must be made: a choice which is at least harmonious with the lines of the Rune Poem, which is consistent with ancient Germanic lore, and which does not fly off into the realms of New Age fantasy. I readily confess that my own interpretation is heavily influenced by "Futhark", written by Edred Thorsson (Dr Stephen E. Flowers) nearly forty years ago. After a number of false starts, this was the first worthwhile book that I read on the subject of esoteric runology back in 1986. In it, Edred threw himself wholly behind the 'lot-box' interpretation and boldly[18] stated:

"Perthro is a cultic symbol for the force of örlög

---

18 Edred (Dr Flowers) now considers "Futhark" to be the least worthy of his published works (though, after all, it was his first, and that is how things should be). He has since written 'ALU: an advanced guide to operative runology" (Weiser, 2012), a much more circumspect work which gives more consideration to all the arguments. Nevertheless, "Futhark" bears the hallmark of a work of *wod*, forged in the flame of inspiration, and I would still recommend it to the beginner.

functioning throughout the multiverse and the way in which men and gods may investigate its workings."

Here it is necessary to explain something about the complex concepts of örlög and of Wyrd. Örlög literally means 'primal laws' or 'primal layers', in the sense of 'that which was laid down long ago'. It is often mistranslated as 'fate', but that is misleading to those who have been raised in a culture largely shaped by Judeo-Christian teachings and classical literature. 'Fate' implies something inescapable, to which one is doomed for an arbitrary reason, such as the whim of a god or goddess. Örlög, on the other hand, represents conditions which have been laid down by past action, and is closer to the eastern concept of karma. 'Wyrd' derives from the Germanic concept of 'becoming', as embodied in the modern German verb 'werden'. Wyrd (Old Norse cognate Urð) means 'that which has become'; like örlög, it is something that has been laid down in the past, and which will form the foundation for subsequent events, conduct, and choices. In Norse mythology, our destiny at birth and throughout our lives is governed by the Norns, the sisters Urð (what has become), Verðandi (what is becoming) and Skuld (what *should* become, based on what has transpired in the past). Our destiny at birth is shaped by the past conduct and actions of our ancestors and, perhaps, our own actions in previous lives. This can constrain us, but in no way is it inevitable, for we can strive against it in the present (see the Need-rune above) to produce a different version of what should be in the future. Changing Wyrd usually happens in small increments, and by mundane actions, but it can be given a powerful kick - in one direction or another - by acts of magic. And, in the end, that is what we are about as operative magicians: bending Wyrd, and changing one possible future for another, according to directed Will.

In Old English, the first line of the verse on Peorth reads "Peorð byþ symble plega and hlehter...": Peorth is always play and laughter. However, if for 'symble' (always) one substitutes 'symbel', a different picture emerges. Symbel - at least in the view of some scholars - was a solemn drinking rite in which the horn was passed around, and the warriors would make binding oaths that they would achieve some great deed or other[19]. This rite has been revived and is practised today by neo-Pagans of the Northern tradition. In making such an oath, ripples are created in the substance of Wyrd; the oath creates örlög and must be fulfilled, otherwise dire consequences may befall not only the maker of the oath, but also those who witnessed it. In esoteric terms, I therefore see Perthro as the outpouring of Wyrd into the world of the present, where it must be endured or dealt with. When using the runes as a method of divination, Perthro can indicate that the situation is governed by past actions or promises, and that one should look to these when considering one's response. In operative magic, Perthro can be invoked to ensure that the working is in accordance with, or designed to modify, existing Wyrd.

Form: ⌐

Phoneme: 'p', as in 'pear'

Number: 14

Esoteric meaning: The outpouring of Wyrd; the decrees of the Norns; past actions and promises working out in the present.

Galdor: p - p - p - p - p *or* pu pa pi pe po

15. ᛉ ELHAZ / EOLHX / ALGIZ

OERP

Eolhx (Elk's sedge) has its home most often in the fen.
It waxes in water and grimly wounds
and burns with blood any bairn
who in any way tries to grasp it.
(Not present in the ONRR or OIRP.)

---

19 See Paul C. Bauschatz "The Well and the Tree" (1982) pp. 72-78 and 110-116 for a discussion of the significance of symbel.

The phonetic evolution of this rune is long and complex - too complex to cover in this brief summation of the runes. Suffice it to say that in inscriptions of the Proto-Germanic era (circa 400 CE), it represents the terminal 'Z' of (primarily masculine, nominative singular) words such as 'MannaZ' (Man). In Old English it was dropped entirely, and was 'recycled' by scribes to represent the Roman alphabet's 'x', while in the northern branch of the Germanic languages the 'Z' ending mutated into a terminal 'R', represented by the Ýr rune (ᛣ).

The original meaning of Elhaz/Algiz is 'elk', i.e. an antler-bearing animal. Stags, harts and hinds are frequently mentioned in Norse mythology. A prized quarry of the hunt, they most probably had sacred status among the Indo-European peoples. Indeed, in Celtic mythology there is even an antlered god, Cernunnos. Elhaz is the protective, apotropaic[20] rune of choice in the Futhark. Its very form suggests the antlers of a stag or an upraised hand with palm outward and fingers spread - in itself a powerful and archetypal apotropaic gesture. The stanza in the OERP speaks of a sharp-leaved sedge that will cut anyone who tries to grasp it, which again has a protective character: fens and marshes, where the sedge thrives, have often provided a refuge for hard-pressed warriors, including Alfred the Great and Hereward the Wake.

The form of the rune (ᛉ) passed into the Younger Futhark as the sign for the Maðr-rune (Man, humankind), and Edred Thorsson also sees in it a symbol of the upward striving (compare Odin's sacrifice of self to Self) that marks the best human quality: the attempt to become *as* a god, even though we are bound by mortality.

In modern, magical practice among runers, Elhaz is frequently used to sanctify and protect the bounds of the Wīh or Vé (temple) at the commencement of a rite or working. It is also the posture (standing, arms upraised) to be adopted when raising one's own wōd or addressing the gods. When

---

20 Warding against evil.

creating a protective talisman, Elhaz should almost always be included.

Form: ᛉ
Phoneme: terminal 'z'
Number: 15
Esoteric meaning: Elk, stag's antlers, or upraised hand; protection, sanctification; communication with non-human sentient beings.
Galdor: a whirring zhzhzhzhzhzhzh, somewhere between 'z' and the French 'j' as in 'jeu'.

16. ᛋ SOWILO / SIGEL / SÓL

OERP
Sigel (Sun) is by seamen always hoped for
when they fare away over the fishes' bath (= sea)
until the brine-stallion (= ship) they bring to land.
ONRR
Sól (Sun) is the light of the lands;
I bow to the doom of the holiness.
OIRP
Sól (Sun) is the shield of the clouds, and shining glory,
and never (is there) ice.

There are few people, especially in cold or even temperate climes, who are not gladdened by the light of the sun. In contrast to the culture and languages of more southerly folk, the people of the north have always considered the sun to be a feminine entity, sister to a masculine moon. In Norse mythology, the chariots of the sun and moon are driven by siblings; Sunna, the sister, drives the brilliant sun-wain across the sky each day, while her brother Máni performs the same task for the moon at night.

The sun is the constant enemy of ice (Isa), which she defeats as her strength waxes, giving rise to the 'good' part of the year (see Jera above). Not only that, by day she is a constant point of reference for navigators to sail by.

Esoterically, Sowilo is one of the most cheerful and hopeful runes, representing guidance and a release from constraint. Despite the apparent similarity of the Old English 'sigel' and the modern German 'Sieg', Sowilo does not stand for victory, though it may be invoked to provide a guiding light, as it were, towards one's desired end.

In magical operations, Sowilo can be used to raise the mood and bring hope in a dark situation, to 'melt' and dispel constraints, and to obtain divine guidance.

Form: ᛋ, ᛌ
Phoneme: 's'
Number: 16
Esoteric meaning: Sun; hope; (divine) guidance; release from constraint.
Galdor: sssssssssssssssss
This ends the second *aett* of the Elder Futhark.

17. ᛏ TIWAZ / TĪR / TÝR

OERP
Tīr is a token, it keeps troth well
with noble men; always on its course
over the mists of night, it never fails.
ONRR
Týr is the one-handed among the Aesir;
the smith has to blow often.
OIRP
Týr is the one-handed god, and the leavings of the wolf,
and the ruler of the temple.

Tiwaz/Týr is the only rune in the Futhark rows which bears the exact name of a god of the northern pantheon, as found in the Eddas. One might expect from this that it would be easy to discern the nature of the rune; unfortunately, this is not the case, as few tales or even direct references survive. Much is therefore based on inference.

The Roman historian Tacitus, writing in the 1st Century CE, said that the three prime gods of the Germanic peoples were Mercury, Mars and Hercules. Of course, Tacitus was interpreting these in terms which the Romans could readily understand, and he is taken to have referred to Woden, Tiw and Thunor respectively. Some confirmation of this is given by the fact that the Roman *dies Martis* (day of Mars) was interpreted as Tiuwesdag (Tuesday) when the Germanic peoples adopted the seven-day Roman calendar sometime between 200 CE and 600 CE. A third-century votive stone found at Housesteads in Northumberland, England, has an inscription referring to 'Mars Thingsus' or 'Mars of the Thing. The stone was dedicated by Frisian auxiliaries stationed on Hadrian's Wall, and the Thing was, of course, the Germanic name for an assembly at which the law was upheld and promulgated. Further evidence of the connection between Tiw and the Thing comes in the alternate Germanic translation of *dies Martis* in Old Saxon as Thingesdag or 'Thing Day', from which the German *Dienstag* and the Dutch *dinsdag* are derived. Týr is mentioned occasionally in the Poetic Edda and the Prose Edda, but except for one incident is not a major player. The incident in question is the binding of the wolf Fenrir, the monstrous offspring of Loki and the Etin Angrboða. As a young pup, Fenrir amused the gods, but he quickly grew to a gigantic size, casting a shadow over Asgard, and eventually only Týr was brave enough to feed him. The gods decided that Fenrir must be bound before he became completely impossible to control. Even this they had to do by trickery, presenting the act to Fenrir as a test of strength. Twice they bound him, and twice he broke the fetters. For the third attempt, they used a dwarf-forged, magical fetter. Fenrir was suspicious of the smooth, silky ribbon, and demanded that before he would be bound by it, one of the gods must place a hand in his mouth as a pledge of good faith. Only Týr was brave enough to give this pledge, and when the wolf strained and shook but was unable to break free, he realised he had been tricked and bit off Týr's hand at the wrist. That is why Týr is always known as the one-handed god. In the Prose Edda, Snorri Sturluson has High-One (Odin) say to Gangleri:

> *"There is also an Ás[21] called Týr. He is the bravest and most valiant and he has great power over victory in battles. It is good for men of action to pray to him. There is a saying that a man is ty-valiant who surpasses other men and does not hesitate. He was so clever that a man who is clever is said to be ty-wise. It is one proof of his bravery that when the Aesir were luring Fenriswolf so as to get the fetter Gleipnir on him, he did not trust them that they would let him go until they placed Týr's hand in the wolf's mouth as a pledge. And when the Aesir refused to let him go then he bit off the hand at the place that is now called the wolf-joint [wrist], and he is one-handed and he is not considered a promoter of settlements."*

The Old English Rune Poem appears to refer to the Pole Star, the prime nocturnal reference point for navigators in the northern hemisphere. There is also reliable linguistic evidence that the name Tiwaz or Týr is derived from *Dyeus*, the Proto-Indo-European sky god whose name is also remembered in the Greek pantheon (Zeus), the Roman pantheon (Jupiter, or Djous-pater) and in the Latin word 'Deus', meaning simply 'God'. Indeed, 'týr' appears to have been an Old Norse word for 'god' in many contexts, for Odin himself has by-names such as Veratýr (god of men), Farmatýr (cargo god) and Fimbultýr (mighty god).

Based on the above attributes, most Runers today see Tiwaz as the rune of a god who presides over battles and lawsuits, and has the power to grant victory in these. He is also a wise god, and as steady and reliable as the north star. Furthermore, he represents altruistic self-sacrifice for the greater good. It is wise to remember, however, that Týr is not, *cannot* be, an even-handed god, and Snorri explicitly says that he is not considered a promoter of settlements. Victory can go

---

[21] A god of the family of the Aesir. (See *Ansuz*.)

to one side only, and woe to the conquered! Before invoking this rune, you had therefore better be very sure of your case. If an amicable settlement is desired, it is better to pray to Forseti (or Fosite), the god of justice and reconciliation. The form of the rune may be derived from Týr's more ancient role as a sky-god, suggesting as it does the dome of the sky supported by the vertical axis mundi or world-column.

Form: ↑
Phoneme: 't'
Number: 17
Esoteric meaning: The god Týr; victory in war or legal matters; wisdom; constancy; altruistic self-sacrifice.
Galdor: t - t - t - t - t *or* tu ta ti te to

18. ᛒ BERKANO (OR BERKANA) / BEORC / BJARKAN

OERP
Beorc (Birch) is without fruit; just the same it bears
shoots without seed; it has beautiful branches
high on its crown; it is finely covered,
loaded with leaves, touching the sky.
ONRR
Bjarkan (Birch) is the limb greenest with leaves;
Loki brought the luck of deceit.
OIRP
Bjarkan (Birch) is a leafy limb and a little tree
and a youthful wood.

At first sight, this rune simply refers to a common tree, with which most people are familiar. As one digs deeper, however, a more complex symbolism emerges. 'Björk', not 'Bjarkan', is the normal Old Norse name for the tree, and 'Bjarkan' probably indicates the name of a Birch-goddess. It is likely etymologically connected with Berchta, or Perchta, a goddess of the Alpine regions of Germany and Austria. Jacob Grimm viewed Berchta as a southern Germanic version of

Frau Holle, and it is esoterically significant that the B-rune holds the 18th position in the row: a multiple of 9 (see the ninth rune Hagalaz above). Birch and Berchta are both derived from the Proto-Germanic word *brehtaz* (shining), alluding to the white bark of the tree and the white skin of the goddess. In many cultures, the birch tree symbolises renewal, reproduction and new beginnings. In the Czech Republic, for example, birch saplings and boughs are used to decorate the streets at Easter. Although it does not produce an edible fruit, the birch reproduces via its catkins which distribute the miniscule seeds on the wind. As a result, it is often the first tree species to recolonise an area after it has been cleared by some natural agency or the hand of man. Iceland, when it was first discovered by Norse settlers in the 9th Century, was largely covered by birch forests - at least in those areas where anything at all could grow. There may also be a connection with the Dutch and German word 'bergen', which has the connotations of 'save', 'salvage', 'conceal' and 'contain'. I therefore personally see the rune as a very protective one that is good for hiding objects - or yourself - from harm.

Form: ᛒ
Phoneme: 'b'
Number: 18
Esoteric meaning: Birch-goddess; inception; new growth; reproduction; concealment; containment; protection.
Galdor: b - b - b - b - b *or* bu ba bi be bo

19. ᛗ EHWAZ / EH

OERP
Eh (Horse) is, in front of the warriors, the joy of noblemen.
A charger, proud on its hoofs when, concerning it, heroes

-

wealthy men - on war-horses exchange speech,
and it is to the restless always a comfort.
(Not present in the ONRR or OIRP.)

Ehwaz, the reconstructed Proto-Germanic word, is cognate with the Latin word 'equus'. As in all ancient, horse-owning societies, Germanic nobles were fiercely proud of their mounts and competed to establish who had the best, even setting stallions to fight against each other. Whether you rode a stallion into battle or undertook long journeys on a sturdy pony across an unforgiving landscape, it was important to ride well and to know the qualities of your steed. The rune describes the beneficial synergy between horse and rider: they are two beings working as a single unit, and anyone who has reasonable experience of horse-riding will know of the joy to be had when horse and rider interact perfectly, each knowing what the other expects. By extension, it can also describe the synergy between two people, such as close friends or life partners, when they have a healthy and harmonious relationship. Each aware of the other's strengths and weaknesses, they can exploit the former in a positive way and compensate for the latter, producing a formidable union that outstrips the simple sum of the two; a kind of 1+1=3, if you like. At the psychological level, the same applies to the interaction between the conscious and subconscious. The conscious part of our mind is capable of logical thinking and rational discernment, but its focus is narrow, like the beam of a flashlight in a dark room. It also tends to be easily distracted and is soon exhausted by sustained analytical thinking. The subconscious, on the other hand, is like the horse element of the horse-rider combination: powerful, tireless, but less focused with its 360-degree vision. It is in the subconscious that many of our deepest fears and anxieties reside, and our most detrimental habits (just as horses are often spooked by innocuous items such as an empty crisp packet). However, with good training of the conscious mind (for the rider must first master himself!), the fears, anxieties and bad habits can be faced, understood and turned around. The enormous strength of the subconscious can then be harnessed and made to work to the benefit of the integrated magician. This is why meditation and ritual are essential to the training of the aspiring sorcerer (see Raiðo above).

At a very basic level of sorcery, I have found that the rune can also be invoked for physical stamina when you feel your strength is ebbing. This came to me when I was on a long walk; my legs were tired, and I wished that I had a horse to ride. In the absence of a physical horse, I projected the Ehwaz rune onto my legs, with the upper angles at my hip joints, and immediately felt a surge of energy which carried me on easily for the last two miles.

Form: ᛗ
Phoneme: 'e', as in 'egg'
Number: 19
Esoteric meaning: Synergy; partnership; harmonious relationships; stamina.
Galdor: eeeeeeeee as in the central 'e' of 'men'.

20. ᛗ MANNAZ / MAN / MAÐR

OERP

Man (Man, humankind) is in his mirth dear to his kinsman,
although each shall depart from the other;
for the lord wants to commit, by his decree,
that frail flesh to the earth.

ONRR

Maðr (Man, humankind) is the increase of dust;
Mighty is the talon-span of the hawk.

OIRP

Maðr (Man, humankind) is the joy of man, and the increase of dust,
and the adornment of ships.

Mannaz describes the human condition. By and large, we are eminently social and tribal beings, and are unhappy if deprived of human company for a long time. This is why solitary confinement is still used as a punishment in prisons (unless for the inmate's own protection) and, even then, has to be used sparingly as it can lead to mental disorders, self-harm and even suicide. We also depend on other humans for social and economic support, and it is a rare person who can happily exist in complete isolation. Humankind is also defined by its mortality; though we may rejoice in each other's company, we must ultimately be parted by death, and our mortal bodies will return to the dust of the earth to feed new growth. The hawk of death constantly hovers over us; we know not when it will strike, only that it will strike eventually. Many people fear the separation which death brings, and the loss of a loved one is often felt as a tragic event. However, mortality is also a kind of blessing, for it gives us a sense of urgency and keeps us sharp. If we are wise, it reminds us to fill our life with purpose and not simply kill time. Another, less well-known rune source, the 'Abecedarium Normannicum' or 'Alphabet of the Norsemen', gives another important clue regarding this rune. In translation, it runs as follows:

ᚠ fee first,
ᚢ urus after,
ᚦ thurs the third stave,
ᚫ the Ase above him,
ᚱ wheel is written last,
ᚲ then cleaves canker;
ᚼ hail has ᚾ need,
ᛁ ice ᛅ year and ᛋ sun;
ᛏ Tiu ᛒ birch and ᛘ man in the middle;
ᛚ water the bright,
ᛦ yew holds all.

The rhyme states that man [is] in the middle, though the rune clearly does not hold the middle place in the rhyme. Rather, it refers to mankind's place in Midgard, the 'middle enclosure'. This is the plane of manifest physical existence which holds the central position in the overall structure of the world tree Yggdrasil. I consider Midgard as the gaming-board on which the influences of all the other worlds and beings are played out. To sum up, we have but a brief span of life - the blink of an eye to the (nearly) immortal gods - but it can be a life filled with a sense of purpose and urgency. For thousands of years, philosophers have pondered on the meaning of life, but what matters in the end is that we *have* life; the meaning we give it is entirely up to us. The line in the Old Icelandic Rune Poem "and the adornment of ships" refers to men as the masters and crews of ships: an adventurous role, if ever there was one, and which leads us nicely towards the next rune.

Form: ᛘ (Elder Futhark and Old English Futhorc), ᛦ (Younger Futhark) or ᛏ (alternative Younger Futhark form

Phoneme: 'm', as in 'man'

Number: 20

Esoteric meaning: Humankind; sociability; companionship; mortality; the physical plane of Midgard.

Galdor: mmmmmmmm

21. ᛚ LAGUZ / LAGU / LÖGR

OERP

Lagu (Water) is to people seemingly unending
if they should venture out on an unsteady ship,
and the sea-waves frighten them very much,
and the brine-stallion does not mind his bridle.

ONRR

Lögr (Water) is [that] which falls from the mountain, a waterfall;
but gold objects are costly things.

OIRP

Lögr (Water) is a churning lake, and a wide kettle,
and booming ground.

Laguz describes water and the principle of fluidity at every level throughout existence, from the fluids coursing through your body to the vast seas and oceans. Water is one of the key elements of ancient proto-science, and is an important factor in Nordic cosmogony: the rivers flowing from Niflheim gave rise to the primal Ice which encountered the Fire of Muspelsheim, to initiate creation. Seas and rivers, boats and ships were very important to our Germanic ancestors, whose heartland first centred on the Baltic coastal areas of Sweden, northern Germany and the Danish archipelago. The sea can be a barrier, true, but for the daring and adventurous it is a highway. Rudyard Kipling summed it up well in his poem 'Jubal and Tubal Cain':

> *"Jubal sang of the new-found sea*
> *And the love that its waves divide -*
> *But Tubal hollowed a fallen tree*
> *And passed to the further side."*

Depictions of ships feature prominently in the Bronze Age rock carvings of Scandinavia. In later centuries, the Germanic peoples of the Baltic and the North Sea were to refine their shipbuilding skills, leading eventually to the tumultuous expansion of the Viking Age when Scandinavian raiders, traders and explorers sailed the North Atlantic to America and navigated the rivers of Russia to Constantinople. In Norse mythology, there are three main entities associated with the sea: the Vanic god Niord (Njörðr), who rules over coastal waters; the Etin Aegir - the northern Poseidon - who rules over the deep seas; and Aegir's wife Rán, who uses her net to drag ships and sailors down to her submarine realm. It is said that Rán is hungry for gold, and sailors would often carry a small piece of gold (in the form of an earring, for example) so as to be sure of a welcome if they met such a fate.

In all the Rune-poems, the image presented is of dynamic and turbulent fluidity. It is a good analogy for life itself, with all its ups and downs, sometimes plain sailing and sometimes downright frightening. To sail the waters, you need a steady ship that answers to the helm, which is to say that you need to be steadfast and in control of yourself. In magic, Laguz can be used in any situation where fluidity is involved or needed. In healing, it governs the fluids of the body, such as blood, lymph and urine. For protection when travelling by sea, use a bindrune combining Laguz and Elhaz. In runic divination, it can indicate turbulence ahead, as when paddling through white water. If you feel the need to calm the turbulence, Isa is a good antidote.

There is another aspect to this rune. Based on inscriptions, some name it 'Laukaz', which means 'leek' in the broadest sense, i.e. all green plants and not only the familiar modern vegetable of the onion family. This is a symbol of vitality and virility, and was sometimes used in kennings for other objects such as swords (battle-leek).

Form: ᛚ
Phoneme: 'l', as in 'leek'
Number: 21
Esoteric meaning: Water; fluidity/liquidity; powerful flow; turbulence; travel across water; challenge; need to be steadfast.
Galdor: lalalalalalala

22. ◆ INGWAZ / ING

OERP
Ing (Ing, a god) was first among the East-Danes
seen by men, until he again eastward
went over the wave; the wain followed on;
this is what the warriors called the hero.
(Not present in the ONRR or OIRP.)

Ing, Ingvi, Yngvi or Ingwaz is another, probably older, name for the god more familiarly known as Frey. As Frey means 'Lord', the god's full title is Yngvi-Frey, or 'Lord Yngvi'. Ing was an important ancestral god of the Germanic tribes residing close to the North Sea in the 1st Century CE, in modern Denmark, northern Germany and the Netherlands. Tacitus, in 'The Germania', refers to these as 'Ingaevones', a major subdivision of the Germanic tribes. Ing was also a major deity for the Swedes, being worshipped at Uppsala, and may even have lent his name to the English. Here I shall treat the names Ing and Frey as interchangeable, since both refer to the same god. The Prose Edda tells us that Frey is a Vanic god, the son of Niord and brother to Freya. At the conclusion of the great war between the Aesir and the Vanir, hostages were exchanged and Niord, Frey and Freya came to live among the Aesir. To Frey was given Liosalfheim, the Home of the Light Elves, as a realm to rule over. Frey is primarily a god of peace, increase, prosperity and fertility. Images of him were generally priapic, indicating his importance in human copulation and reproduction. Another eponym for Frey may have been Fróði or Frode (Wise), which brings an association with the harvest (see the ONRR for *Jera* above). An image of Frey used to be carried from settlement to settlement on a wain, or cart, and this is reminiscent of the end-of-harvest processions which were common until comparatively recent times, when a mannequin composed of the last sheaves of corn was carried on a wain through the community amid general rejoicing. One aspect of Ing is therefore cognate with John Barleycorn, the god who is constantly slain but always rises again from the seed slumbering in the earth. Esoterically,

Ingwaz represents that seed. The form of the rune (◊) is smaller than most other rune-forms, and is always depicted as floating freely between the two horizontal lines that can be used as guidelines for the others. As the seed resting in the earth, which in time will burst forth under the influence of

Berkano to give the harvest (ᛒ), it represents the principle of latency and of latent power. It is a good rune to use in operative magic when you wish to store power - for example, in a talisman that you wish to activate only when necessary. Ing can also be invoked when the magician needs a period to rest and recoup, and in divination it can indicate that something hidden is brewing: perhaps an early pregnancy.

Form: ◊ or ᛝ
Phoneme: 'ng', as in 'sleepi<u>ng</u>' or 'E<u>ng</u>lish'
Number: 22

Esoteric meaning: The god Ing/Frey; increase; prosperity; fertility; peace; latency / latent power.

Galdor: ing - ing – ing

23. ᛞ DAGAZ / DAEG

OERP

Daeg (Day) is the lord's messenger, dear to men,
the ruler's famous light; [it is] mirth and hope
to rich and poor [and] is useful to all.

(Not present in the ONRR or OIRP.)

In Norse mythology, Day is a natural phenomenon personified, as can be seen in the words of the Valkyrie Sigrdrifa when she was awakened by Sigurd:

> *"Hail Day! Hail, sons of Day!*
> *Hail Night and her kin!*
> *With gracious eyes may you look upon us,*
> *And give victory to those sitting here!"*

For our Germanic ancestors, night was always considered as preceding day, and they counted the passage of time by nights, as can be seen in the term 'fortnight' (fourteen nights) for a two-week period. 'Sennight' (seven nights) was also formerly also used for a single week, but has now fallen out of use. In the Prose Edda, High One relates that Night was the daughter of an Etin named Narfi, and that she was black and dark. She married thrice, and her last husband was Delling, who was of the race of the Aesir:

> *"Their son was Day. He was bright and beautiful in accordance with his father's nature. Then All-father took Night and her son Day and gave them two horses and two chariots and set them up in the sky so that they have to ride around the earth every twenty-four hours. Night rides in front on the horse called Hrimfaxi, and every morning he bedews the earth with the drips from his bit. Day's horse is called Skinfaxi [shining-mane], and light is shed all over the sky and sweat from his mane."*

The Day-rune describes not only the bright part of the day between sunrise and sunset, but the entire 24-hour cycle of night and day. It is a rune which depicts the synthesis of the opposites of dark and light. The form of the rune may be considered as similar to a Moebius strip, with one polar extreme constantly transforming into the other at the central point. Dagaz is a rune of liminality, of those paradoxical moments, like dawn and dusk, when one stands at the edge between one thing and another, and nothing is either one thing or another, so everything is possible. This is where the magic occurs, for as well as being the best time of day to perform magical operations, it is also a mindset that can be achieved, with some training[22], at any time of day.

Form: ᛞ
Phoneme: 'd', as in 'day'
Number: 23
Esoteric meaning: Polar opposites synthesized; transformation; liminality
Galdor: d - d - d - d - d *or* du da di de do

24. ᛟ OTHALA / ODAL / ETHEL

OERP
Eþel (Estate) is very dear to every man,
if he can enjoy what is right and according to custom
in his dwelling, most often in prosperity.
(Not present in the ONRR or OIRP.)

Othala is the principle of heritage, inherited property, and inherited rights and customs. It describes all those things which are handed down to a person from his or her ancestors. It can be added to (and, unfortunately, devalued), but unlike

---

[22] "Alice laughed. 'There's no use trying,' she said. 'One can't believe impossible things.'

'I daresay you haven't had much practice,' said the Queen. 'When I was your age, I always did it for half-an-hour a day. Why, sometimes I've believed as many as six impossible things before breakfast.'" - *Alice in Wonderland* by Lewis Carroll.

Fehu (mobile wealth) it can never be alienated outside of the family, tribe or nation. While it does include your home and property - if you are fortunate enough to own your own home - that ceases to be your *Odal* if it is sold instead of being passed on to your progeny. When a person dies and the question of inheritance is sorted out, we speak of the dead person's estate. However, the rune covers more than just land and property, for it refers to your heritage in the broadest sense: culture, language, customs, genetic inheritance and fatherland - everything which makes you what you are, but is shared with others of the same heritage and background. However, ancient rights also bring ancient duties, whatever our station in the family, tribe or nation. Now, as an old man and the head of a family, I am reminded of the dictum *noblesse oblige* - nobility brings duties - but as a youngster I was an upstart, did not yet understand the duties, and had to be slapped down time and again; now I can understand why this was necessary. In my own (very personal) interpretation, I see Othala as 'holding' all the other runes of the Futhark row, as the runes are our heritage, passed down to us via Rig from Woden.

Form: ᛟ
Phoneme: 'o', as in 'b<u>o</u>th'
Number: 24
Esoteric meaning: Estate; heritage; immovable property; ancient rights and customs.
Galdor: ooooooooooo as in 'open'
This ends the third and final *aett* of the Elder Futhark.

This completes our introduction to the 24 runes of the Elder Futhark. As already stated, readers are strongly encouraged to read other works on esoteric runology, and references for these are given in the bibliography. My principle is that I only write a book if I can add something new and germane; I don't do 'me too' works or write simply in order to jump on a bandwagon. Do read books by different authors (preferably at least three) so that you can gain different insights and form a critical opinion. However, you should not feel confused or disappointed if one author appears to contradict another. The runes are frequently paradoxical and will reveal themselves in different ways to different people. And now it is time for them to reveal themselves to you!

CHAPTER 4

TAKING UP THE RUNES

In verses 138-139 of the Hávamál (Lay of the High One), part of the Poetic Edda, Odin tells of his exemplary, self-sacrificial deed of hanging himself on the World-Tree in order to gain knowledge:

> *I know that I hung on the windy tree*
> *Nights of all nine, wounded by the spear*
> *And given to Odin, myself to myself*
> *On that tree, of which no man knows*
> *From what root it rises.*
> *They gave me no bread, nor drinking-horn.*
> *I looked down; I took up the runes;*
> *Screaming I took them!*
> *And fell back from there.*

This has to be the most inspiring passage of all for those who have dedicated themselves to learning runelore and applying it. In effect, Odin gives his entire existence as a sacrifice to himself; he puts himself through an extraordinary ordeal to transcend the being which he previously was. It is an ecstatic experience, for he screams (or roars) as he seizes the runes and makes them his own. After that, he goes on to say that he gained more and more knowledge:

> *Then I began to grow*
> *And waxed well in wisdom.*
> *One word led me to another,*
> *One work led me to another.*

Of course, no-one is asking you, as an aspiring magician, to hang yourself on a tree and run yourself through with a spear in order to gain the necessary knowledge, but it will be necessary to offer up some time and effort. You will need to put aside the normal distractions of modern life, such as TV and the social media, for a short while every day as a sacrifice from the person you were to the magnificent demi-god that you can be. If you are already consistently performing the exercises prescribed in Chapter 2, this will feel like no burden at all; all you need do is to introduce the runes into your daily fun.

You can start by taking a blank sheet of paper and a pen or pencil, and practising writing the runes. Refer to Chapter 3 as often as you need to, or to Appendix 2 which summarises the runes, to get the forms right, and write them in the correct order. Though they will feel unfamiliar at first, you will soon find it as easy as writing the common alphabet in capital letters. When you feel confident enough, create a pack of 24 white cards of uniform size. Playing card size is ideal, and packs of blank playing cards are commercially available. However, you can just as easily create cards from used cereal packs if you don't have the money to spend. My own solution was to use somewhat thicker and more durable board to create cards 3 inches by 2.5 inches (7.5 x 6.5 cm) in size. I still have these and sometimes use them for divination. On each card, write a single rune, beginning with Fehu and working through to Othala. They should be written using a felt-tip marker or coloured pencil in red (or whatever colour suggests power and energy to you).

Exercise 8

First, read aloud to yourself the Rune Poems for Fehu and place its card in front of you. Fix the image ᚠ in your mind's eye. As you did previously, adopt a comfortable position that you can maintain for 20 minutes, breathe steadily without straining, and empty your mind of everything but the rune. Every time you breathe out, utter the rune's galdor; in this case "Fffffff". Visualise the rune glowing bright red against a black background. Continue this for about 3 minutes (you don't need to set a timer), then lapse into silence. Think about the various aspects of the rune - its shape, sound and number - and allow your mind to explore its deeper meaning for the rest of your 20-minute session. If you should find your mind wandering off course, guide it back by resuming the visualisation and utterance of the sound. After you finish, write down your thoughts, insights and impressions in your diary.

When you have done meditating on Fehu in this fashion, you can move on to Uruz and continue through to Othala. You should preferably devote 3 daily meditation sessions to each rune before moving on to the next, but there is no hard-and-fast rule for this. You may well find that you grasp some of them quickly, while others tend to elude you and need more time. The main thing is that you continue to actively seek out the runes and their applications throughout the waking day. For example, you may handle a coin, bank note or debit card and think "Fehu!" or see a sudden shower of hail and think of Hagalaz. When you have a few moments of spare time, practise instantly clearing your mind and focusing on a rune, its meanings, and how it relates to other runes and the world at large. In this way, you will quickly find that the runes start to speak to you. Another thing you may find is that the rune-forms appear to you in a colour other than red, and that each acquires its own, specific colour association for you. For example, to me Gebo is green, Wunjo is violet, Jera is straw-yellow and Perthro is grey. It is best not to force the issue: simply allow each rune to spontaneously manifest itself in the colour it chooses. Do, however, check whether the colour manifestations are consistent or transient. Again, make notes and consider what the colour means to you. It is yet another channel by which the rune is attempting to communicate with you.

Another rewarding exercise is to draw 3 cards at random from your pack, lay them before you, and consider how they relate to each other. What story do they tell? Performing this exercise on a daily basis can enormously enhance your ability to 'read the runes' if you wish to use them for divination.

Carving

You should already be familiar with the rune-images from your practice at writing them and producing your own set of cards. Although the Futhark runes and the Icelandic magical staves were frequently written on parchment or paper from the 16th century onward, the runes were originally designed to be carved on wood or stone - hence the angular forms with no horizontal lines. If you carve a horizontal line on a wooden tine, it will simply disappear into the grain. Carving the runes into wood (which many runers refer to as 'risting' from the Old Norse verb *að rista*: to cut) is something you should learn; firstly because it is deeply satisfying, and secondly because it endows the magical intention with greater permanence and 'solidity'. To do this, you will of course need a good, sharp knife. In the old Icelandic grimoires, many spells instruct you to carve a stave using your *mathnif*, or 'food knife'; before modern table cutlery, everyone carried his or her personal knife for cutting food, and it was most likely a general-purpose tool, always at your side. Many modern magicians in the Northern Tradition like to obtain rather large knives in the style of the Anglo-Saxon *seax* for their magical work, but I do not advocate this. They are far too big and unwieldy to be held like a pen. Furthermore, carrying such knives tends to be frowned upon by the police these days, and could land you with a charge of carrying an offensive weapon. My own preferred solution is to purchase a new, folding pocket-knife that has at least one small blade and one large one. The Victorinox range of Swiss Army knives is excellent for this purpose. You should give your knife a name and reserve it entirely for your own use - never lend it to anyone! This will be the first item in your magician's toolbox, to be added to in due course.

As your first exercise, go out and find one or more twigs about one inch (2.5 cm) in diameter and about 12 inches (30 cm) long. Split them lengthways with the large blade of your knife or, if this proves impracticable, scrape away one side of the twig to produce a flat surface to carve on. You can now practise carving the runes, taking care to carve across the grain of the wood. You might need to practise this several times, but the acquired skill will be useful later when it comes to making talismans and other objects. Note that your carved runes will not show up very well on the blank wood; you will have to stain them to see them properly. We will come to methods for staining and colouring in the next chapter when we talk about the magician's toolbox and its contents, but for now you can take a pinch of clay or loamy soil in the palm of your hand, wet it with your spit and rub the resulting mud into the cut runes. Wipe the tine with a damp rag or tissue, and the runes should now show up nicely. Using soil and spit in this way should not be thought of as less magical than other, more elaborate methods. It is replete with symbolism, and a perfectly valid method when you have nothing else. As you will see, I take a minimalist approach to magic and eschew the idea that you need a cart-load of paraphernalia to make it work.

Note that many of the old Icelandic spells use the word 'carve' when they mean something quite different. For example, "Carve this stave on your left palm using your right index finger and the water from your mouth" clearly means that you should wet your finger with spittle and trace the stave on your palm. Magical staves might also be clipped into the fur or wool of livestock to heal or protect them. If you are into pyrography, you can try burning the runes into wood, which produces a different but pleasing effect and empowers them with the element of Fire.

Projecting

Also referred to as 'signing and sending', this is an extremely powerful technique that can be used anywhere, without tools, to project runic force across vast distances if necessary. All you require are your own visualisation and breathing skills. Begin by standing or sitting up straight, breathing calmly and deeply (without forcing), and emptying your mind. As you inhale, visualise a ray of brilliant, white light emanating from a point infinitely far above you, coming down and entering your body through the crown of your head and penetrating to your solar plexus. Maintain this image as you inhale again and visualise a ray of black light emanating from infinitely below you, rising upward and entering through the soles of your feet (or your buttocks if you are sitting) and joining the white ray in your solar plexus. See them swirling together and feel their interaction. Now visualise rays of bright, red light coming in horizontally from distant points to your front, back and both sides at chest height. See and feel them joining within you at the same point, your solar plexus, where the white and black light meet. Continue to breathe steadily, picturing the movement of your breath, both inward and outward, fanning the combined energy like the bellows of a forge to make it shine with incandescent heat. Now, touching the first two fingers of your dominant hand to your solar plexus, 'draw out' the energy like a ribbon of blinding, multicoloured (white/red/black) light and trace the form of your chosen rune in front of you. As you do so, sing out the name of the rune (e.g. Thurisaz) and see the rune being painted, as it were, on your target. Your target may be an object or person that you can physically see, and is therefore relatively close; if not, then you will have to visualise your target as well; or you may prefer to have a symbolic image of it, such as a drawing, in front of you. I find it helps to end the projection by thrusting at your target with an open palm, as if you were physically throwing the rune.

Perhaps a practical example will help here, something that will be of immediate use to you. It is time to go to bed and, in addition to the usual precautions of locking doors, you want to employ some magical energy to ward your home. In addition, it would be nice to always have joy in your abode. You think on the runelore that you have learned and select Othala (ᛟ) to represent your home, Elhaz (ᛉ) for protection, and Wunjo (ᚹ) for joy. Stand facing the main entrance of your home, draw the energy into yourself in the manner described above, touch your fingers to your solar plexus and then 'paint' the image of Othala on the inside of the door, followed by Elhaz and Wunjo superimposed on it. As you do so, intone "Othala - Elhaz - Wunjo!", if possible in a single breath. The resulting visualised bindrune should look like this:

HOME-WARDING BINDRUNE

When you have completed the signing and sending, give a long exhalation, release any residual stored energy, and disconnect yourself from the external sources you employed; see those rays of light leaving you and disappearing back in the directions they came from. We will come back to the finer points of magical operations later, but two things are important to remember at this stage:

1) Never use your own energy; always draw the magical energy into yourself from your surroundings and then project it;

2) Always consciously disconnect yourself from the energy after you have used it, and put the deed behind you.

When I was first learning how to use rune magic, I was trying very hard to make a living as a reflexologist. At the end of each session, I would hold the patient's feet in my hands and 'donate' some energy to them. The patient usually felt the benefit but, as should have been obvious in retrospect, I rapidly depleted my own energy and became prey to depression and anxiety until another alternative health practitioner, an osteopath, pointed out where I was going wrong. At the time, I was reading Edred Thorsson's book 'Futhark' and putting its lessons into practice, so I applied these lessons to my reflexology sessions. Before donating energy, I drew it in from the four quarters, from above, and from below, and then gave the patient half of it. The rest I kept for myself. The result was a net gain for the patient while I was able to maintain the charge in my internal, magical 'battery' instead of depleting it. The other thing that this wise and experienced practitioner taught me was to sever the psychic connection between me and the patient as soon as the session was over with the conscious act of washing my hands. Naturally, I washed my hands anyway for reasons of physical hygiene, but the act now became a small ritual of separation. I soon felt better and more energetic, and stopped worrying about the patients in-between sessions.

Avoiding overload and obsession

Everyone is different, and for this we should be thankful. It would be a very dull world if we were all to respond identically to every stimulus and situation! It goes without saying that different readers will respond differently to the challenge of the exercises I have set out so far. Some may find them tedious, while others will find them stimulating and enjoyable. Some will perform them diligently every day, but others will do them intermittently, and some may make a start but quickly forget to do them at all. It is really up to you: all I can do is present a method and leave it up to the reader how far he or she wishes to take it. No-one else can do the work for you. Thus far, I have worked from the assumption that the process of magical awakening will take some effort, and that the effort will ultimately prove beneficial, rather like a commitment to get a little more physical exercise each day, or to alter one's daily schedule in a way that gives more productivity. However, it must be recognised that we are dealing with extremely powerful magical forces, and that there is a danger of imbalance. The runes are more than willing to communicate with those who open up the channels of communication, which can, in some individuals and circumstances, result in overload. This usually manifests itself in the form of intense dreams, a tendency to think about the runes in every minute to the exclusion of all else, and an inclination to talk obsessively about the subject with all around you. You may find that you feel fidgety and unable to relax, or unable to concentrate on anything for a sustained period. Conversely, you may start to feel drained and exhausted, or start to act and think in way that is uncharacteristic of you. Change can be a positive thing - and it is to be hoped that your efforts will bring positive benefits to your life and attitude - but it is essential to maintain a balance. Fortunately, there are ways to avoid such symptoms or to counter them should they arise.

- Take a break. Every week, take one day off and devote no attention whatsoever to magic. If you start to feel overwhelmed by the results, take a longer break until you feel calmer and more stable;
- Listen to what others are telling you. You certainly don't need to discuss your magical progress with others - even close family - let alone allow them to read your magical diary. If you live in an intolerant environment, it may be better to say nothing. Meeting for the first time with other people who are equally interested in magic and are keen to discuss it can be an absolute joy. On the other hand, if people let you know that you are boring the pants off everyone around you, it is time to take notice and review your behaviour;

- Take physical exercise. Intense mental activity should always be balanced by physical activity. Only you can assess your relative level of physical fitness, but whether you take a walk, play a game of tennis, or have an intense work-out at the gym, it should be regular and enough to raise a sweat and make you slightly out of breath;
- Remember to practise thinking of nothing. This was your very first exercise, and can easily be forgotten!
- Refer to your magical diary and read it as if it were the diary of a third person. What impression would that person make on you?

Rune-work can be tremendously exciting and beneficial. You may find yourself making new connections and discoveries every day, and will perhaps experience an urge to express yourself artistically in prose, poetry or the graphic arts. You may also find that pleasing 'coincidences' and synchronistic occurrences are happening in your life. If you feel happy and well, and your life is proceeding to plan, then all is well and good. If you feel unhappy and imbalanced, and things are not going to plan, it is time to take a break, review matters, and implement the countermeasures listed above.

CHAPTER 5

THE MAGICIAN'S TOOLBOX

We will soon be looking at some full-on magical work, set in a ritual context. By now, you should have the most important tools - a basic knowledge of the runes and the skills of carving, signing and sending - but there are some bits and pieces that you will require in order to perform northern magic in an authentic and traditional way. Practitioners of magic in some other traditions, presumably inspired by venerable grimoires such as the 'Key of Solomon', advise beginners to acquire a vast array of physical tools and accoutrements such as a custom-made altar, a sword, a dagger, a wand, various bowls, a pentacle (i.e. a tablet inscribed with a pentagram symbol), candles, an incense burner, and ornate banners. The assumption seems to be that every aspiring magician has the house room for all this kind of stuff and will only ever be performing operative magic within the confines of a dedicated temple. I am not saying that this approach is wrong in itself, and it can be fun if you have a deep purse and a love of theatre. The point is that you do not *need* them. If necessary, you can perform entire rituals with only the visualisation of all the aforesaid implements, and the end result will be just as effective. On the whole, I am a big fan of magical minimalism, 'empty-handed magic' if you like, which requires only the use of your own mind, body, gestures and voice. Magic, to be of any use, needs to be available as and when you need it. You may frequently have time to plan ahead and perform a perfectly composed ritual using all of these beautiful items; sometimes, however, you may find yourself stuck at midnight in a strange town after the buses have stopped running, and your luggage is on the other side of town. That's when you *really* need some effective sorcery!

Herein lies the attraction of magic in the old Icelandic style. It was folk magic, assembled and performed by people who were living at subsistence level and who had to cobble something together using whatever came to hand. I will not be including every possible item here, as some are hard to come by these days, and others are so impractical that one wonders whether they were ever truly used. Instead, I will confine the list to basic items that are readily available today. You should already have two things that will be of use to you: your magical diary, and the small knife that you used to carve the runes. You can extend your diary to include certain spells, or you can get a new, blank book for the spells alone. I like to keep a 'Book of Deeds' as a record of my practical operations. In it I log every magical working, starting with the situation which requires a magical solution, progressing through all the associated considerations, and eventually arriving at the exact form of the working and its results. As for the knife, it should be small enough to be legally carried in your pocket or in a small pouch (not sheath) on your belt at most times. You can and should use it for any purpose you see fit; when it becomes your constant companion, its power will be all the greater, and it will develop more character.

You can begin to collect your tools immediately, but before long you will need something to contain them, especially the smaller items. This should be big enough to hold them, but small enough to be comfortably carried using one hand only and - if necessary - conveniently hidden from prying eyes. This is in accordance with the minimalist tradition of Icelandic magic: if you find yourself acquiring so much 'stuff' that you need a suitcase and eventually a wardrobe, then you might want to consider another path such as that of the Golden Dawn. Continual acquisition of physical paraphernalia de-focuses the mind and often becomes a hobby (or vice) in itself. A small, wooden box is ideal; my own measures 12" x 8" x 7" (30 x 20 x 18 cm). If you have some carpentry skills, you can make your own and embellish and decorate it to your taste; if not, such boxes are widely available on the commercial market and are often very attractive. Alternatively, you could use a leather or canvas satchel if you expect to carry your kit around with you often. Again, you can make your own, but commercially produced models are widely available and not very expensive. My own solution is to have both: the aforementioned wooden box together with a small, canvas satchel just big enough to carry the few magical items that I might need on a daily basis (plus my wallet, keys, and several poop bags for our two dogs). So let us move on to the list of prosaic, yet at the same time, wonderfully magical things that will be going into that box or satchel.

- You will need a few candles. Magic works best in the absence of artificial light and, moreover, the lighting of a candle evokes the element of Fire and the rune Kenaz, kindling and quickening your magical will and focusing your mind on the business at hand. For the most part, simple, stubby tea-lights will suffice. A half-dozen of these can easily be stored in your toolbox, and a single tea-light can be carried in your satchel. They do not cast much downward light, however, so you will need to include one or more standard 8-inch (20cm) candles to provide illumination when you are writing or risting something without the aid of natural light. You can also, if you wish, store some coloured candles for various uses, and it is good to have some miniature candles in the colours red, black and white for ritual purposes. On the other hand, please don't be obsessive about this; aim to be able to work with a single candle or even none at all.
- Matches. Well, that should be obvious, really, as you need something to light the candles with. The main thing is the factor of kindling through friction, representing the rune Nauðiz. A lighter will also suffice, as long as it strikes iron against flint.

- Incense cones or joss sticks. These are not really essential, and they are not prescribed in any of the northern grimoires, but I do find that the scent of incense helps to focus the mind, immediately establishing a distinct 'other-worldly' atmosphere which divorces your proceedings from the mundane routine. You need to include a small metal plate to stand the cone on, or a wooden holder for a joss stick; these are usually included in the purchase. Avoid really cheap stuff (which sometimes smells like burning tyres).
- Scriber. This is a sharp tool made of hardened steel, and is used for making marks on metal. You can also use it as an awl when traditional spells call for the use of one.
- Whetstone. You will need this to sharpen your knife, and spells are given later on to make it more efficient. Get a small one - you only need to sharpen a pocket-knife, not a scythe!
- Pens and inks. You can, if you wish, use the traditional nib pens and bottled inks. These have a satisfying, antiquarian feel to them but do require a little skill to get pleasing results. Personally, I find it more convenient to use fine felt-tipped or rollerball pens, and these are available in a variety of colours. Have red and black as a minimum.
- Chalk. Some of the old spells call for magical staves to be written in chalk, and it is in any case an excellent medium for writing on large, rough surfaces such as stone or wood.
- Compass, protractor, rule and set square. You will sometimes require these in order to draw your own staves neatly, and compact sets are cheaply available from stationery stores.
- Paper. We take this so much for granted these days, using reams of the stuff and receiving far more of it in the post than we would wish, but this wonderful material revolutionised written communication.

Before it became widely available, the only available material for books and scrolls was parchment made from animal hide. Being expensive, it was often reused, with the old writing being scraped away. When I was first learning about magic, I used to see old texts calling for signs to be written on 'virgin parchment'; it took me a long while to realise that what they meant, in effect, was 'a blank sheet of paper'. Always keep a few slips of blank paper in your toolbox. You can, of course, use genuine parchment if you can get hold of it, though I doubt the magical bonus will be worth the expense.

- Various other materials on which to carve staves, if you want to follow the old instructions to the letter. For example: offcuts of brass and lead, slips of wood from various tree species, and the thin, papery bark shed by the silver birch. In fact, anything you find on your travels which you think may find a magical use sooner or later. Materials that you have found or begged will always feel more interesting (and hence hold more power) than those that you bought with cold, hard cash. I was fortunate to have a local shop which made trophies, and managed to beg a few pieces of scrap brass and, when neighbours were having their roof repaired, I begged a couple of sheets of old lead flashing from the workmen. When collecting odd twigs of wood for future use, make a mark on them to remind you what kind of tree they came from! Oak, rowan, birch, beech, alder, pine and red spruce are all mentioned in the old Icelandic grimoires. You can also save any old pieces of broken gold and silver, such as a broken chain. If you have gold crowns or fillings then, whenever these need replacing, insist that the dentist returns the old one to you. Such scraps of precious metal can be useful as offerings.
- A wooden bowl for scrying. This will probably not fit into your box or satchel, but it can be useful if you have

any skill in scrying. Filled with water, it fulfils the role often otherwise taken by a crystal ball or black mirror. Some of the scrying spells call for yarrow to be scattered on the water; yarrow (*Achillea Millefolium*) is a herb commonly found on grassy lawns. The best thing is to pick it when the Moon is full, dry it, and then grind it fine using a mortar and pestle.

- Divination bone. The knucklebones of sheep have been used for thousands of years for divination and gaming, and were used in Iceland. I was given one by a friend on my first visit to Iceland, and always keep it with me. The bone has a 'hump' on one side and a 'hollow' on the other; decide for yourself which side means 'yes' and which means 'no', and be consistent in this. It can also fall on its side, which indicates that no decision is possible at the present time.

MY OWN TOOLBOX AND SOME OF THE ITEMS THAT RESIDE WITHIN IT

Note that I have not included a wand. There is no mention of wands in the old Icelandic books of magic. I have one, but I find I do not actually use it much these days, finding that I generally use one or more fingers to fulfil the same role. If you feel moved to own a wand, then have one that you can proudly carry in public and use for another purpose, i.e. a walking stick. Even if you are young enough to walk without the aid of a stick, they are useful and, moreover, completely legal weapons for self-defence. I have such a stick, inscribed in runes with boasts of my magical achievements, and very useful it is, too. Nor have I mentioned a bag of wooden, stone or metal rune-staves for divination. This is because such an item also does not feature in the books of magic, and may indeed never have been used in the old days. The only divination methods mentioned in the Icelandic grimoires are scrying and oneiromancy (divination by dreams). However, do not let this deter you; if you wish to divine by means of a rune cast, then go ahead and make your own set of lots. I must confess that I use that method frequently. Whatever you do, make your own implements insofar as possible, for they will prove far more powerful than anything bought in a shop.

Hallowing your magical tools

Tools which are used frequently in your magical operations, and used for nothing else, will tend to become hallowed (sanctified) by use over the course of time. However, you may wish to cleanse them of past associations and dedicate them to their new purpose before using them for the first time. The same applies to items which are used in your operations on an incidental basis (see Chapter 13 on Sendings) and therefore cannot be hallowed by frequent use. The following gives a simple but effective rite of magical cleansing. You will need:

- Two small bowls, one containing water and the other a pinch or two of salt;
- A candle (this can be your usual altar candle);
- Burning incense;
- The object you wish to cleanse.

First, take a pinch of salt, drop it in the water, and then stir the water with your finger until the salt has dissolved. Then take the thing that is to be hallowed and hold it aloft (if possible) and say:

> "Behold this thing of Midgard, having all the virtues and vices of this realm of Man. Let us take it and make of it a thing that is fit for use in the service of the Gods, and by us as we sacrifice self to self, following the holy way of Odin!"

Sprinkle the item with the salted water and say:

> "I cleanse thee by Earth and Water!"

Passing the item through the incense smoke, say:

> "I cleanse thee by Air!"

Pass the item over the candle flame and say:

> "I cleanse thee by Fire!"

Then raise the index finger on your dominant hand to Asgard (above your head), draw down the brilliant, holy light of that realm, and sign an equal-armed cross over the object, saying:

> "I cleanse thee in the names of Odin, Baldur, Frey and Thor!"

If the item is to have a specific purpose, you can then pronounce its doom (purpose or mission).

A word on dressing up...

Many aspiring magicians suffer from what I call 'Rincewinditis', after the character Rincewind in Terry Pratchett's Discworld books. Rincewind, an undergraduate at the Unseen University, is not actually very good at magic, so he makes up for it by wearing a tall, pointed hat with the word 'Wizzard' embroidered on it in sequins. Some traditions of magic positively encourage the wearing of robes, sashes, hoods and funny hats. Others, conversely, advocate the wearing of nothing at all except for some fashionable occult jewellery. The point of doing this is to separate oneself, mentally and emotionally, from the hum-drum world of everyday life, to tell yourself that this situation is different, and that you are ready to perform magic. At base, you should still be able to practise magic efficiently when you have not even had a decent wash or a change of clothes for a while: perhaps the more so, for magic is most needed in adverse circumstances. It may be safely assumed that the Icelandic sorcerers of old wore their everyday clothes when engaged in magical operations. However, it does no harm to have a sense of occasion when possible, as when one dresses for a formal dinner or for a job interview. It is therefore a good idea, when preparing, to take a shower or bath[23] (or at least a good flannel-wash) and put on clean clothes. Better still, you might wish to reserve a certain combination of clothes for use only when you are performing magic. They need not be outlandish or even specially procured, just clean clothes that are in good repair. They can be in a special colour or colours that you associate with magic, whether plain black, or colourfully patterned, or any combination in between. Many magicians like to use a specific gesture to signal to themselves that they are about to start using magic. They might, for example, turn a signet ring around or expose a certain amulet. You may even find yourself doing this instinctively. In Njal's Saga, the wizard Svanur perceives that enemies are seeking out his kinsman. He wraps a strip of goatskin about his head before uttering words to summon mist and fog, thereby causing the enemies to lose their way. It may well be that Svanur used this strip of goatskin to signal to himself that he was about to commence an active magical working.

---

23 See also Chapter 15 on washing rituals.

CHAPTER 6

RITUAL MAGIC

What is ritual? At the mention of it, most people will think of solemn ceremonies of a religious or secular kind, with words, actions and gestures performed in a time-hallowed and immutable sequence. Take, for example, a Mass, a Royal Coronation or the Trooping of the Colours. In fact, we perform rituals routinely and unconsciously throughout the day, from tying our shoelaces to driving a car. Our daily rituals involve words, actions and gestures which we once had to learn and perform consciously, but can now perform automatically with barely a conscious thought. Ritual is governed by the rune Raiðo (R) and has the beauty and benefit that it brings us automatically into a certain state of mind which can then be maintained with little further effort. Consider the processes of your mind as you prepare to make a journey in your car: up to the point of opening the car door, you may have all kinds of extraneous thoughts but, once you sit in the driver's seat, a considerable part of your brain-power automatically 'switches on' and devotes itself to the necessary sequence of actions; seat belt, ignition, check dashboard ("Darn, nearly empty... need to get fuel"), check mirrors, engage gear and so on. You have become an actor in a role that you have performed hundreds of times before, with a script that you could utter and perform in your sleep. In exactly the same way, we can bring ritual into magic, enabling ourselves to be smooth and fluid in its performance. The ability to carry out key actions, make certain gestures and utter significant words and phrases by rote liberates the conscious mind to focus on those actions which are crucial and peculiar to the magical operation. This is why you, as an aspiring magician, should first enact magic in a ritualised manner. Think of this learning process as similar to your first driving lessons, or - even longer ago - being taught to tie your shoelaces. Those things did not come easily at first, but now you do them with ease.

You already have the necessary tools and skills for operative magic, to wit:

- The ability to still your mind, empty it of extraneous thoughts, and focus on the matter in hand;
- The ability to visualise and synthesize images, sounds, scents and tactile experiences;
- A basic knowledge of rune-lore;
- The ability to project, write and carve runes.

All you require now is a ritual framework that will endow these skills and this knowledge with pattern and direction, so that they can be employed to make changes in subjective and objective reality - in other words, to change yourself and the world around you. In due course, after discussion of the main techniques of Icelandic magic, you will be given a worked example which will cover most, if not all, eventualities. In the meantime, let us work towards something simple to enhance your daily exercises. Like any good story, rituals have a beginning, a middle and an end. We will refer to these as the Opening, the Working, and the Closing.

The Opening

This is the section of the rite in which you set the stage and get into your role as the magician. To begin with, there are certain physical aspects which must be taken care of. Some of these were dealt with in the previous chapter, but others are introduced now. The main considerations are time and space. You need some time when you will not be disturbed by anyone. Turn off your mobile 'phone or set it to 'do not disturb'. Evenings and early mornings generally work best, as there is less external activity. Now and again, you may need to perform a rite at a certain time, on a certain day, or at a certain phase of the Moon, but we will come to that later. As for space, choose somewhere uncluttered if working indoors. Having a dedicated room in your home is ideal, but few of us have that luxury. In the more likely situation that you are using your living room, dining room or bedroom, then make sure that it is as clean and tidy as possible. You can also work outdoors if you have a place where you are unlikely to be interrupted or spied upon by strangers. The place where you perform your ritual magic will henceforth be referred to as your 'stead', from the Icelandic word 'staður', a place.

The focal point of your activity should be your altar or, as we call it in the northern tradition, 'harrow' (from the Old Norse word *hörgr*). This can be a dedicated, specially constructed item, or it can be any convenient, flat-topped item of furniture which will fit the bill. A coffee table will serve well. If you have to use something which forms part of your everyday furniture, then take care to obtain a special cloth to cover it, thereby separating its mundane function from its sacral function. The cloth can be of any colour or material you choose; personally, I prefer one of black cotton. Black has the advantage that it does not distract, and does not so readily show scorch or ink marks. Cotton is a natural material and, unlike polyester, does not sustain as much damage from the small sparks emitted by self-igniting charcoal blocks if you choose to use those. It goes without saying that this cloth effectively makes your harrow, and it should be used for nothing else. The harrow serves two functions. At the practical level, it is your workbench for the crafting of talismans and other magical items. At the esoteric level, it serves as a bridge or link between your inner, subjective world and the outer, objective world of magical reality. If you are in the northern hemisphere it should usually reside on the northern side of your stead, facing the Pole Star. In the southern hemisphere, it should be oriented towards the south. The aim, in either case, is to align your consciousness with the Axis Mundi, the trunk of the World-Tree Yggdrasil. On the harrow you will need:

- At least one candle or tea-light with a suitable holder or insulating mat. One or more standard candles in tall holders are useful to provide illumination if you are working in a darkened room. You will also need matches or a lighter to light them with.
- Some source of incense. This can be a joss-stick, an incense cone, or a pot full of sand[24] with a charcoal block in it, plus loose incense;
- The written words with the order of ceremony and the words you have to recite. These can be contained in a book, on a sheet of paper, or on postcard-size cards. I find that the latter are most convenient as they take up least room. As you progress, you will be able to memorise many of the frequently used formulae, and will only require these 'flash cards' for the material that is unique to a particular working;
- Pens, slips of paper or anything else you may need; for example, to create a talisman.

Having prepared everything, approach your harrow reverently. Stand before it for a minute or two and put all else out of your mind. Taking nine deep breaths, visualise a sphere of power in scintillating, sky-blue light extending all around you and delimiting your working space. It separates you from the mundane world and defines your stead. Note that this sphere should extend below the floor and your feet as well as above and around you. As you approach the ninth breath, visualise above you a pool of blinding, white light: this is the light emanating from Asgard, the home of the Aesir. After completing the ninth breath cycle, reach upward with your dominant hand, grasp the light and draw it down to the crown of your head, touching your forehead with your thumb, chanting as you do so the name "Vé!" See the light blossom

---

[24] Make sure to use non-combustible sand or gravel. I once filled my pot with peat-based soil, which soon started to smoulder and filled the room with an unwelcome amount of smoke! It will not help your ritual if you have to break off to fetch water to douse your harrow.

into an orb emanating from the crown of your head. Now draw the light down further, to your throat, chant "Odin!", and see the light blossom in an orb around your throat. Having done that, draw the light down still further to your solar plexus and chant "Vili!", seeing the light pulse and emanate from your solar plexus. Next, keep hold of the power, draw it to your right shoulder and chant "Huginn!" Visualise a shining, white raven on that shoulder. Now draw the powerful light across your upper chest to your left shoulder and chant "Muninn!" and, likewise, visualise a shining white raven on your left shoulder. Take another deep breath, then exhale as you expansively spread your arms wide. See a pulse of energy, like the shock wave from an explosion, radiating out from you and exerting your will on the world around you. Then inhale deeply as you bring your hands in again to cross them on your chest, drawing in all the power and magic of the world and absorbing it into yourself.

Now draw a match from the box (or take up the lighter) and hold it at arm's length above your head to remind you that the kindling first takes place by the power of Asgard. Lowering it again, strike the match or lighter while uttering "Nnnnnn!" (ᚾ, the rune of kindling) and then light the candle(s) while saying "Candles, kindle, and so quicken my cunning". Meditate for some seconds on the power of the rune Kenaz (ᚲ), the controlled fire. Subsequently, light your source of incense, whether it be a joss stick, incense cone or block of self-igniting charcoal (you will have to put resin-based incense on the latter once it is glowing well). As you do so, say:

> "These holy herbs and resins, heaped upon the fire[25],
> send smoke, most wholesome, pleasing to the gods but
> driving dire things far, far away."

---

[25] Of course, you don't literally heap them on the coals if you are employing the more convenient (and portable) sticks or cones, but it does not hurt to say the same words and remember that this was the method used of old!

When your incense is smoking properly, carry it sun-wise around the perimeter of your stead, saying three times

"So hallow I this holy stead; worrisome wights wend away",

then put it back on the harrow.

Finally, stand in the centre of the stead facing north. Maintaining the visualisation of the scintillating, sky-blue sphere all around you, and the white light pouring into you from above, visualise also rays of bright red light emanating from an infinite distance at each of the four quarters (north, south, east and west), plus a ray of black light extending upward from deep below your feet. Picture and *feel* all these rays - red, white and black - conjoining and swirling within you at your solar plexus. Take three deep breaths and visualise the fiery power of the rays being fanned by each inhalation and exhalation, as charcoal is fanned to white heat by the bellows of the smith's forge. Touch the first and second fingers of your dominant hand to your solar plexus and draw out this incandescent power, ready for projection. Extending your arm, project it towards the northern boundary of your stead like the blinding beam of a lighthouse and trace the stylised form of Thor's hammer as in the illustration below.

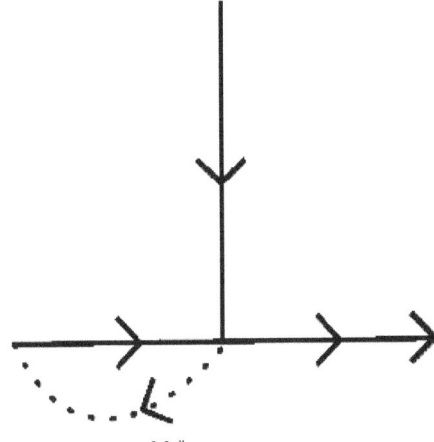

MJÖLNIR SYMBOL

As you do so, say in a commanding voice "Mjölnir[26], hallow and hold this holy stead!" Turning sun-wise with arm still extended, repeat this for the other three quarters, without lowering your arm, until you are facing north again and have created a complete circle with Thor's hammer at each of the four quarters. Then, still facing north, sign and send the same symbol above and below you using the same words.

To finish:

(Standing with arms outstretched to your sides) say

"About me..."

(Bring your arms inward so that your fingers touch at the solar plexus)

"...and within me..."

(Stretching upward with your hands and then lowering them to touch your forehead)

"...Asgard..."

(Lowering hand to touch solar plexus again)

"...and Midgard."

This completes the opening rite. It may appear rather long-winded, but in practice it takes rather less time to perform the above than it does to read it. When you are used to practising it on a daily basis, you will be able to complete it proficiently within a few minutes, devoting little conscious thought to the mechanics and focusing instead on the meaning - which, after all, is the benefit of ritual.

Let us pause for a moment to think about what we have just done, for it is replete with symbolism that may evade the beginner. First of all, you have invoked the three primal gods, the brothers Odin, Vili and Vé; you have literally drawn them down into yourself. To invoke means 'to call in'. They were always within you, in any case, for you are the hybrid offspring of god and man but, where they were previously dormant, they are now awakened. Note that I use the sequence Vé-Odin-Vili instead of Odin-Vili-Vé. I deem this

---

26 Pronounced 'Mee-URL-neer'.

appropriate as Vé stands for holiness, and his proper microcosmic station is at our highest physical point, the crown of the head. Odin is master of speech and language, and I therefore place him at the throat and the larynx. Vili, whose name means 'will' I place at the solar plexus, for it is in the heart region that we perceive our will and courage ('courage' being derived from the French word 'coeur', or heart). On our right and left shoulders respectively rest the two mythic ravens of Odin, Huginn and Muninn, whose names mean 'mind' and 'memory', so we awaken these aspects of our soul-complex in ourselves. I picture them as shining white rather than black because this image spontaneously came to me early on in my own ritual practice; I believe it to be a perception of their inner essence.

When you strike the match or lighter, you should begin to hum "Nnnnnnn" a couple of seconds before the action of striking. The kindling, by friction, thereby becomes an evocation of the N-rune, Nauðiz, thereby multiplying the kindling factor for your entire rite. The same applies to the fourfold 'k' phoneme that you make as you utter "<u>C</u>andles, <u>k</u>indle, and so <u>q</u>uicken my <u>c</u>unning!" and light the candles. It has the effect of sanctifying and empowering an otherwise mundane act, and awakens the controlled flame of Kenaz, in your stead and within yourself.

The words spoken when burning the incense are a recognition of their dedication to the gods - an offering - and an affirmation of their warding effect against any malign wights which may be present. This is reinforced when you cense the perimeter of your stead, hallowing it and driving away malign influences.

The signing and sending of the symbol for Mjölnir, the hammer of Thor, is widely used by modern rune magicians and is known as the Hammer Rite. It evokes the power of that mighty weapon, which Thor wields in order to protect Midgard and Asgard against the forces of chaos and destruction, so that the 'universe' of your stead may be similarly protected. And, upon completing this rite, you assert that all of Midgard and Asgard are about you and within you

- a powerful assertion of your ability to command affairs and events everywhere, as a demi-god.

Experienced runers will immediately recognise that the above opening rite and its components are inspired by the work of Dr Stephen E. Flowers (a.k.a. Edred Thorsson), as published in his seminal work 'Futhark: A Handbook of Rune Magic[27]' and 'The Nine Doors of Midgard[28]', and I am in debt to his influence. Purists will no doubt object that the rite is a modern invention, which it is. To that I respond that no written or even oral accounts survive concerning the rites performed by Icelandic magicians in the Mediaeval and Early Modern periods in preparation for their magical operations. As I commented in my previous book, 'Icelandic Magic', the Icelandic grimoires or *galdrabækur* more resemble the random kitchen notes of forgotten cooks than the masterworks of leading chefs. We therefore have to be inventive.

The Working

This is the core part of the operation, when you set about doing what you came here to do. It could be to create a talisman, to sign and send runes or a magical stave (*galdrastaf*) to a given target, to create a sending, or to perform an act of divination. At first, you may simply wish to use the ritual setting to invoke a certain rune, or combination of runes, and meditate on them. There are so many options that it would be pointless to dwell further on the subject at this point, but suffice it to say that the objective of any working is to *change the narrative*, i.e. to re-write the story that you are living in. To this end, it is often useful to find a story from mythic narrative that resonates with your purpose, and to incorporate a short reading of it into your ritual. You thereby align your working with the primal, mythic narrative and endow it with greater strength. This is one of the reasons why you need to be thoroughly familiar with Norse mythology. The most

---

27 See Bibliography.
28 See Bibliography.

important thing in a magical operation is to *have absolute confidence that your efforts will be effective*. Put all doubts aside. See the results of your working as *already having taken place*, and already a fact.

The Closing

The final part of the ritual is devoted to ending it cleanly and effectively, so that you leave behind a neutral space with no lingering magic or entities, feeling calm, collected and confident that your magical operation has been successful. Fortunately, it is shorter and much more straightforward than the opening.

The first thing to do is thank and dismiss any entities (gods and/or wights) whom you may have evoked in the course of the working, in reverse order to the order in which they were evoked. I would suggest a simple, bold statement as follows:

> *"I thank you, (Name), for attending these rites. Go now in peace, and let there always be peace between us."*

Secondly, you must declare the operation to be at an end. I find the final verse of the Hávamál (Lay of the High One) from the Poetic Edda to be highly effective here. Stand before the harrow, facing north, with arms outstretched at your sides and recite:

> *"Now are Hár's sayings said, in Hár's hall;*
> *Needful for the sons of men*
> *But unneeded by Etins' sons.*
> *Hail to the one who spoke them,*
> *Hail to the one who knows them,*
> *Useful, to the one who took them;*
> *Hail, those who heed them."*

Then, bringing your hands together before you, declare:

> *"So be it. The rite is ended."*

Lastly, you must decide what to do with the power that you may have amassed in the course of the working. There are two basic options, depending on the intention of your working: you can internalise it, or you can release it. If your working was intended to bring about a change in yourself, or consisted of a passive operation such as divination, it is best to draw the generated power into yourself. You can do this as follows. Face north and extend your arms at your sides, then sweep your arms inward until your hands overlap on your solar plexus. As you do so, declare "Æpandi nam![29]". Turning sun-wise, repeat this for the remaining three quarters. If your working was directed towards bringing about an external change (i.e. to work on a person, object or situation elsewhere), then it is best to simply 'slash' the boundary of your stead with your knife or the edge of your hand in the appropriate direction. Visualise the sphere rupturing and the power pouring out to have its intended effect.

Upon completion of such a ritual, you will often notice its mental and physical effects on yourself. You may feel exhilarated, or drained, or a combination of both. It is not unusual to feel warm to the point of sweating, even though the ambient temperature may be normal. Notwithstanding, you should clear up immediately, snuffing the candles and dousing the incense if it cannot be left to burn out safely. Put away all magical paraphernalia in the place where they normally reside (your toolbox or satchel). To 'earth' yourself and regain a feeling of normality, have a drink and something to eat (tea and biscuits are my preference) and write up all your experiences in your magical diary. In the days, weeks and perhaps even months to follow, do not dwell on the result of your working. Do your best to put it out of your mind completely. If you dwell on it, you will constantly call its energy back to you and fritter away its power. Naturally, it is reasonable to review things after an acceptable interval has

---

29 Pronounced "Eye-pandi nam". This is a phrase from Hávamál 139, meaning "Roaring, I took them up!", and refers to Odin's gaining of the runes as he hung on the World-tree.

passed. For example, if your intention was to gain inspiration, has your artistic output increased in quality and quantity? If the intention was to resolve a difficult situation, what are the signs that this has happened? Once you have allowed a reasonable amount of time to elapse, you can record the results in your diary. Try to be objective and record them honestly; only in that way can you hope to learn from your experience and improve as a magician.

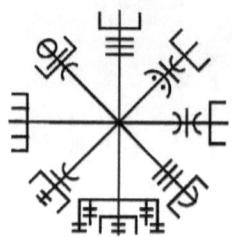

PART 2:
THE TECHNIQUES OF RUNIC AND ICELANDIC MAGIC

In my book "Iceland Magic: Aims, Tools and Techniques of the Icelandic Sorcerers", I wrote in great detail about the techniques of Icelandic magic, based on a thorough analysis of six surviving books of magic. What I did not do - to the disappointment of some readers - was explain concisely how these techniques might be put into practice. The aim of the present book, therefore, is to make good that omission. Some reiteration will be necessary, so if you have already read that book, please bear with me.

Magical spells in the northern tradition most commonly employ one or more of the following elements:

- An appeal to supernatural entities such as the gods of the Heathen pantheon and/or the Holy Trinity of the Christian faith;
- An incantation or statement of intent;
- A graphic element in the form of one or more runes, magical symbols (*galdrastafir; singular galdrastafur*) or magical images (*galdramyndir, s. galdramynd*);
- Delivery of the formed spell to its target.

The first three elements may be employed singly or in combination, but frequently all of them are involved. We shall consider each element separately before bringing them together to form a template for our magical operations.

CHAPTER 7

APPEALS TO SUPERNATURAL ENTITIES

Religion is an unfashionable topic these days, at least in the so-called 'advanced' countries of the western world. With increased prosperity and urbanisation, materialism has steadily relegated religious faith to the back seat, and faith in mechanistic science has replaced ancient folk beliefs and customs.

Even three centuries ago, professed religion and church attendance had often become a matter of political convenience, and the confirmation of social customs and standing, rather than a profound and considered assertion of one's relationship with the Godhead. Even where religious tenets are adhered to, those tenets tend to be only proscriptive and are often obeyed more out of fear than for the sake of joy. To be fair, the Enlightenment era followed centuries of religious warfare and fanaticism, in which people had butchered and tortured those who followed other faiths, and even those who did not adhere to their own narrow interpretations of the Bible. And, on the bright side, the Enlightenment was followed in the latter 19th Century by a reaction, a new quest for supernatural meaning by minds that were able to look outside the confines of orthodox religious belief. This resulted not only in an exploration of eastern beliefs and practices, but also in a revival of interest in the indigenous religious beliefs held by our Germanic and Celtic forefathers before the priests came from Rome to tell them that they lived in error. Not only that, it allowed for a culture in which antiquarians could study and catalogue such folklore as had not already been neglected or extirpated. Such things can only benefit those of us who would learn from the past in order to construct and implement northern magic for the present day.

One must bear in mind that, by 1500 CE, Iceland had been nominally Christian for a full five centuries. Despite that, belief in the existence of the old Heathen gods proved very persistent, even though they may not have been actively worshipped. The Icelandic spells of the early modern era frequently have appeals, in some form or other, to supernatural entities. Such appeals are often implied or low-key, such as the inclusion of 'IHS' (In Hoc Signo) in a *galdramynd*, or a requirement to recite a piece of near-meaningless dog-Latin such as a highly corrupted element from the Latin version of the Lord's Prayer. Occasionally, however, they include overt (and sometimes lengthy) appeals not only to God, Christ, the Holy Spirit, Mary and the saints, but also to older, Heathen gods such as Odin, Thor, Baldur and Freya, and sometimes the Elves.

It is my own view that it is beneficial to nurture a symbiotic relationship with the gods and other intelligent but non-human denizens of our world. We, the humans, are ephemeral beings, for the most part as transient and insubstantial as a wave on the strand, unless we pack our lives with memorable deeds or - better still - work to ensure that our essence will survive death and be reincarnated, eventually becoming god-like ourselves. The gods, on the other hand, are almost immortal, looking down upon us with flinty eyes, as we might deign to look upon the activities of an ant farm. They have immense power, far beyond our ken, but ironically are dependent on our belief for their life-blood. Without that belief, they fade and, when their very names are forgotten, they die, or retreat into the rocks or the wind, to wait until they can find followers again. The Aesir and Vanir (Ases and Wanes in English) are a case in point. Neglected for nearly 900 years except in the folklore of isolated Scandinavian and Germanic communities, they now have a resurgence of belief among the various Ásatrú individuals and communities the world over. In general, you don't have to be Ásatrú to practise Icelandic magic, but it helps[30].

Then there are the other wights (beings) that are not gods but nevertheless are different to mortal human beings: the elves, the dwarfs, the tree-spirits, the rock-spirits, the wind spirits and so on. We also have the wights of hearth and home, some of whom may once have inhabited your home in bodily form and whose spirits have become bound to it. The wights of nature, for the most part, wish merely to be left in peace with their existence untrammelled by human contact: a vain hope for most of them as our species becomes ever more invasive. Nevertheless, many can still be encountered in the open countryside, and even in parks and woods close to urban areas. They vary widely in character, and are known in folklore by many different names, depending on your country or region, so you can make a good start by investigating the traditional folklore of your area. Entire books have been written on the subject, and I can recommend "Elves, Wights and Trolls" by Kveldulf Gundarsson and "The Tradition of Household Spirits" by Claude Lecouteux[31].

So what are these benefits of nurturing a symbiotic relationship with the gods and wights, and how may we go about it? The first and most obvious reason for doing so is that any appeal to them in the course of your magical workings is likely to fall on deaf ears unless a solid, reciprocal relationship has already been built up. As stated in the introduction, we already have kinship with the gods and incorporate a latent aspect of divinity within ourselves, but picture this: if someone comes knocking at your door asking for help, whose request are you most likely to grant? Someone whom you

---

30 On the other hand, it also pays to be eclectic. I have been a Heathen for more than two-thirds of my life, but once I lost my wedding ring (it was not well sized for my finger). My wife and I searched everywhere, and I tried every spell that I knew, to no avail. Eventually, someone suggested a prayer to Saint Anthony of Padua, and I tried that. He came up trumps and I found the ring soon afterwards. On subsequent occasions, the good Saint has helped us find other mislaid items, and we honour him with a candle on his day, 13 June. This is completely within the spirit of Icelandic magic of the early modern period.
31 See bibliography for both of these books.

have never met before, even though they may claim to be a distant relative, or someone who is well known to you, and a trusted friend? It is therefore best to work, quietly but assiduously, on making yourself known in advance to the gods and wights whose assistance you hope to call upon. Another reason for doing this is that your gods will become your friends and allies, teaching you things which cannot be read in any book, and lending you their might when you feel run-down and at the end of your tether. This is not to say that you should blindly worship the gods, or grovel before them; that is not the way of the magician. Rather, you should try to establish an association of mutual respect by demonstrating that you are willing to learn from them and, above all, will strive to *help yourself* by magical means.

There are many gods and goddesses in the Nordic pantheon, and it can be quite a task to get to know all of them. You can make a start by reading the tales of their exploits in the Poetic and Prose Eddas, or in any decent book on Norse Mythology intended for the general reader. An excellent and quite detailed overview, which includes some of the more obscure gods and goddesses, can be found in "Our Troth", Volume 1, published by The Troth[32]. You will no doubt find it easier to form a rapport with some deities than with others, and you may ultimately wish to focus on one or two of them - a god and a goddess, perhaps - while still remaining on good terms with the rest. A concise summary of the major Germanic deities and their attributes can be found in Appendix 4.

As for ways in which you can connect with these ancient and powerful gods and goddesses, you can incorporate some or all of the following practices in your daily, weekly and monthly routines. You may already be doing some of these!

- On rising, take a minute to give thanks for the new day, simply being thankful that you live and breathe.
- Before eating your main meal of the day, join hands with those who share in the meal to bless the food and

---

[32] See bibliography.

give thanks to Frey and Freya (the providers). These are the words we use in our household:

> "We thank the gods for this food. We thank them for all the sources from which it came, and for all the work that brought it to our table. May it be filled with strength, that it may strengthen us in our lives and in our quest for Rúna. So be it!"

- On each day of the week, give consideration to the deity for which it is named: Sunna on Sunday; Máni on Monday; Tiw (Týr) on Tuesday; Woden (Odin) on Wednesday; Thunor (Thor) on Thursday; and Frey, Freya or Frigg on Friday. Saturday is problematic, as the day is named for the Roman god Saturnus[33]. I associate that day with the Norns, but one may also keep it free to allocate to a god or goddess of one's choice. It is also useful, as a break from meditation on the runes, to meditate on one of the gods on the appropriate day and to burn some incense as an offering.
- Before sleeping, give thanks for the day that has been. You can formulate your own words, and the following is only my suggestion:

> "Thank you, mighty gods, for this day that has been, and for all the good things you have given us. Please protect us, and all those we love, this night and always, and our properties too. Give us all we need to be happy and healthy, and where there is not health let it be restored. Help us to be the best that we can be, and to do the best that we can do in everything we undertake, and give us victory in all we undertake. Aesir and Vanir, so be it."

---

[33] The Germanic tribes are thought to have adopted the Roman system of day-names at some time before the fall of the Western Roman Empire, interpreting them in terms of native gods who were cognate with those of the Romans (e.g. Wodanaz for Mercurius). As there is no god in the northern pantheon cognate with Saturnus, it may be that they simply kept the original name. Modern Scandinavian names for Saturday derive from ON Laugardagr (= 'bath day'), presumably being the day when it was customary to take one's weekly bath.

Ever-increasing familiarity with the gods in a vibrant and vital relationship will infuse your ritual appeals with a powerful rush of meaning that is infinitely better than a bald recitation of formulaic words. Gifts are also appreciated; it usually helps to pour a libation of mead, wine or ale after calling on one or more gods to help with your working. (I also routinely reserve the last centimetre from each bottle of wine as an offering. These are collected in a small bottle which, when full, I carry to a mighty oak not far from my home and then empty it against the bole with the words "To the Aesir and Vanir, and the wights of the woods.") It should also be mentioned that, prior to the conversion to Christianity, the old gods were frequently honoured with blood sacrifices. Human customs and ethics have changed over the past thousand years, but the gods remain relatively unchanged. Though I do not advocate animal sacrifices (let alone human!), because they are cruel and messy, you can 'spice up' your offering of mead with a drop of your own blood[34]. I have noticed during my own rituals that the atmosphere can change significantly when this is done. One can sense a feral heightening of interest, as though wolves were sniffing around; the room becomes a little darker, and the presence of power becomes more palpable.

If you intend to include an appeal to a deity or deities in your working - and I do recommend it - it should generally be made directly after the Opening and before the incantation. Try to craft your words to the best of your ability, but if you are no poet and have, as yet, little experience, say simply and honestly "I call upon .... to help me in this working; I offer you this gift", and pour your libation. The choice of deity will very much depend on the intention of your working (see aforementioned appendix), but one can never go far wrong in calling upon Odin to strengthen any act of magic, as he is *par excellence* the master of magic, poetry and inspiration.

---

[34] Not to be recommended when the horn is to be shared with others because of the obvious danger of cross-infection.

CHAPTER 8

INCANTATION

Our modern English word 'incantation' is derived from the Latin verb *incantare*, "to bewitch, charm, cast a spell upon, chant magic over, sing spells", which in turn is based on verb *cantare*, "to sing". The modern Icelandic word for magic, *galdur*, is derived from the verb *að gala*, meaning "to sing or chant", and Old English used the similar word *galdor*. Incantation - words sung or chanted - is at the heart of Nordic magic, and embodies the belief that words and song can create or change objective reality. As stated previously, magic is about changing the narrative, and incantation is the means by which we do this.

Your incantation can be as elaborate as you wish, though sometimes a single word or phrase can suffice if you can pack it with enough power and meaning. An elaborate *galdor* is more useful for major workings in a ritual setting, while terse words, sounds and phrases are more appropriate when you desire instant effects on an ad hoc basis. Here we will work on the assumption that you have the time to plan and carefully craft your incantation.

- Firstly, try if you can to align your intention with the primal, mythic narrative, and include a recitation based on this. The Poetic Edda is a good source for this. For example, if you have been going through something of an ordeal lately and you want to turn things around, you could begin by reciting the verses already quoted from the Hávamál (*"I know that I hung on the windy tree..."* etc. See Chapter 4) and add verse 141:

> *"Then I began to grow*
> *and waxed well in wisdom.*
> *One word led me to another,*
> *one work led me to another."*

The mythic recitation does not have to follow the format of the main body of your incantation.

- Your main incantation should be crafted to the best of your ability, using good rhyme, meter and alliteration. If your poetic ability is weak, it will be worth your while to study the subject and practise penning a few lines daily[35]. Make it something you can chant or, if possible, sing. The tune itself is less important than the mood it conveys.
- The incantation can consist of two sections: a statement of how things have been until now, followed by an assertion of the changed reality that you bring about. The latter part is the more important.
- Keep things in the past and present tenses, for these are the more 'real' tenses. The future always lies beyond the horizon, and if you chant your new reality in the future tense it will always remain in the future and never fully manifest itself.
- Avoid negatives. Your subconscious and the magical universe do not understand words such as 'no', 'not' and 'never'; if you employ them, they will be omitted from the result. For example, if you say (as your magical intention) "I feel no pain", then what you will get is "I feel pain". It is better to turn it around and say "I am well".
- Have great faith! This is a phrase often found in the old Icelandic books of magic. It does not mean

---

[35] Stephen Fry's book "The Ode Less Travelled: A guide to writing poetry" (Arrow, 2007) is very enjoyable primer.

religious faith; it means having utter confidence that your working will be successful. See yourself as an indomitable warrior, an all-powerful wizard, or a combination of both.

When using runes in your working, you can insert the *galdor* for these at certain points while, at the same time, signing and sending the rune forms in the direction of their target or into a magical object that you are creating. There are three main ways to chant a rune-galdor:
1) The rune-name itself, e.g. Fehu: "Feeeeehuuuuu!"
2) The phoneme, e.g. "Fffffff".
3) The phoneme connected with the runic vowels, e.g. "Fu fa fi fe fo"[36].

Other forms of rune-galdor can be found in Edred Thorsson's book "Futhark".

To conclude, here is an example of an incantation you might compose if you feel you have not been duly rewarded for your efforts up to now, and your intention is to have comfort and financial security by invoking the runes Jera (ᛃ), Fehu (ᚠ) and Wunjo (ᚹ).

> "Wondrous wealth is mine by right,
> Fulsome fees I always win.
> My wage is comfort, joy and light,
> Reward and harvest gathered in.
> Jera jera jera!
> Fehu fehu fehu!
> Wunjo wunjo wunjo!"

You can continue intoning "Jera Fehu Wunjo" repetitively as you carve, colour and send your bindrune.

---

36 It is likely that the giant's chant "Fee, fie, fo, fum" in the tale "Jack and the Beanstalk" is a folk memory of just such a formula.

CHAPTER 9

RUNES AND BINDRUNES

The graphic element of your magical operation can be as simple or as complex as you wish to make it, or is necessary to the operation. In general, it is best to go for simplicity; sometimes a single Futhark rune will suffice for your purpose. For example, if you wish to gain wealth, you could create a simple talisman with the rune Fehu (ᚠ) boldly written or inscribed on the one side, and the phrase "ᚠ comes to me" on the other side. When a single rune cannot cover the intention of the working, two or more may be used. These may then be joined by a connecting line at their base or combined into a single monogram. We refer to this as a 'bindrune'. A popular, simple bindrune used for safe travel is a combination of Raiðo, representing the road, and Elhaz, representing protection. These two runes can be either connected by a line underneath them, or they can be combined into a single rune (see illustrations below).

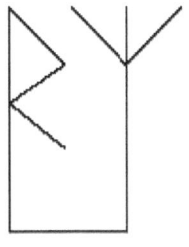

A) CONNECTED FORM

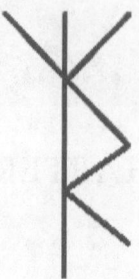

B) COMBINED FORM

This bindrune can be carved or written as a talisman, perhaps to be hung from the rear-view mirror of your car, or it can be projected in an act of signing and sending at the start of each journey. In the old books of magic, the verb 'að rista' - to carve - was frequently used even when staves were written in ink, pencil or chalk, were clipped into the hair or wool of livestock, or were even simply traced on one's own skin in spittle. I shall therefore adopt the same convention and use only the word 'carve'. It is always a good idea to trace out your staves in advance using a pencil. Standard technical drawing instruments such as a compass, protractor and linear ruler can be used to obtain aesthetically pleasing results.

It pays to practise the formation of bindrunes that are balanced, harmonious and attractive in appearance, and you can start by creating a runic monogram using your own initials. To make your monogram or bindrune more balanced and attractive, you may have to reverse the direction they would normally face, or even have them facing upward or downward. In most cases this solution is to be preferred, as your bindrune will have a very lop-sided appearance if all the constituent runes face in their conventional direction. Staves which predominantly consist of a vertical element, such as Isa or Tiwaz, or which radiate from a central point, such as Gebo or the Younger Futhark 'snowflake' version of Hagalaz, can conveniently be used to form an upright or framework on which to 'hang' your other runes. Use them as such if they occur among the runes of your choice, but never introduce them unless they are appropriate to your intention. As you carve a rune, make sure to sign and send it into the carved image at the same time (see the section on 'Projecting' above). That is to say, you must take the power gathered within yourself and see it flowing from your centre, along your arm, into the point of your knife or pen, and then into the shape you are carving.

An extremely important point must be made now. When you create a bindrune by combining the rune-forms (as opposed to tracing a connecting line beneath them), there will inevitably be some overlapping of the staves; the more complex the bindrune, the more overlaps there will be. Consider a bindrune that is intended to bring prosperity, companionship, guidance and joy to your home, in an atmosphere of open and mutual generosity. It will probably contain the following runes:

ᚩ - for the home
X - for giving, generosity
ᚠ - for monetary prosperity
ᛗ - for human companionship
ᛋ - for guidance, plain sailing
ᚹ - for joy

and the bindrune may look something like this:

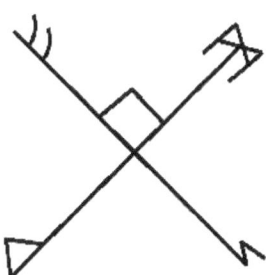

You can see how the vertical elements of Fehu, Sowilo and Wunjo merge with the diagonal strokes of Gebo, and Othala is very much subsumed into Gebo. Only Mannaz has a more or less independent existence, sitting at the termination of one of Gebo's 'arms'. You might therefore be tempted to carve the Gebo rune and then add to it… a couple of strokes here and there to complete four of the other runes, and then Mannaz at the tip of an arm. But no, this is not enough; if you do it that way, your magic will probably not work. *Every* rune must be individually traced, even when it is made to overlap with one or more others. This is less of a problem when signing and sending, which uses only visualisation, but what are we to do when a bindrune is to be carved? Unless the magician has a very steady hand, there will be some deviations from the previously created lines, and the result will be unsightly. The solution, in my experience, is to trace each individual rune but 'ghost-carve' those sections which have already been drawn or carved. If you are using a pen, simply hover closely over the surface for those parts while still singing the rune-name or its phoneme and sending its power into the glyph. If you are literally carving, then just lightly run your knife point along sections that have already been scored without trying to carve them deeper, thereby running the risk of slipping and scoring a parallel line.

Colouring

If you have literally carved runes into a suitable surface such as wood, you will often need to colour them so that they show up. As we can read in the sagas, blood was the traditional medium for several reasons. Firstly, it is readily available - you only have to cut yourself with a sharp knife. Secondly, blood represents the life-force itself, so in colouring a carved rune with your blood you are imbuing it with life-force. Thirdly, it is bright red when fresh, a dynamic and energetic colour, though it darkens to brown when dry. Fortunately, for those who - like me - are averse to shedding their blood in such quantities, there are alternatives which use other traditional materials. Red madder or red ochre pigment can be mixed with raw linseed oil to produce a blend very similar in texture and appearance to blood. Red madder has been used as a pigment for thousands of years, and red ochre has been used even longer, since the Old Stone Age. Linseed oil is pressed from the seed of the flax plant, which is sacred to spinning goddesses such as Frigg and Holda. Another option is to use the juice of berries such as blackberries or elderberries. Whether you use blood or pigment, it is important to sign and send the intended runes into them as you stir, singing the rune names or phonemes. In "Futhark"[37], Edred Thorsson advocates ending this charging procedure with the assertion "Blood of Kvasir[38] be blessed! Rune-might blooms in the blend!"; I fully concur with this, for it produces a powerful mythic connection. Personally, I like to strike a compromise by making a blend of red ochre and linseed oil (a teaspoonful of the latter is more than enough), then (after calling the runes into myself by focused meditation and rune-singing) pricking a finger with a needle and allowing a drop or two of my blood to drip into the blend. If you can get hold of the needles which diabetics use to test their blood sugar daily, you will find that they are extremely sharp and virtually painless. You can also use spittle if you wish; this, after all, also gives something of yourself and has associations with Kvasir. Spittle is frequently used in the traditional Icelandic galdrastafir. Some of the blood or pigment will unavoidably be left on the surface of the tine, outside of the carved runes; this can easily be wiped away using a cloth wetted with a little linseed oil.

Being bright, fiery and energetic, red is the default colour for runes. However, you may find a good reason to paint them in a different colour and therefore use another pigment. Let intuition be your guide here, and refer back to your work on colours in exercise 6b (Chapter 2). Of course, you can avoid the lengthy preparation described above by simply using coloured pens or pencils. I sometimes do this, but it always

---

37 Op cit., p. 112.
38 At the conclusion of the primaeval war between the two races of gods, the Aesir and Vanir, they sealed the peace by spitting saliva into a vessel and fashioning from it a being named Kvasir. Kvasir was said to be very wise, and could answer any question put to him. He roamed the world, teaching mankind, but was lured into a cave and killed by two dwarfs. The dwarfs mixed his blood with honey in three vessels, respectively called Són, Boðn and Óðrærir, to create the mead of wisdom. This was eventually captured and used by Óðinn.

feels less powerful than doing things in the old-fashioned way.

Having carved and coloured your runes or bindrune, you must breathe life into it by holding it close to your mouth and uttering the formula "FA!" with a strong exhalation. This combines the power of the runes Fehu and Ansuz. Finally, take your finished magical object and form an orb of containment around it using your cupped hands. Strongly visualise a spherical field of blue light that will fix the power, but is permeable enough to allow some of it to emanate outward and have its intended effect on the objective world. You can then give it a name, and instruct it in its purpose (doom).

CHAPTER 10

GALDRASTAFIR AND GALDRAMYNDIR

The early modern period (roughly the 16th and 17th centuries[39]) saw, for the first time as far as we know, a profusion of books of magic in Iceland. The Icelandic for a book of magic is *galdrabók* (plural *galdrabækur*). These were private notebooks, hand-written on parchment or paper; some consisting of but a few sheets, but others were more extensive. There is some evidence that the spells they contained were shared with others, and that the books were passed on to new recipients and were even added to - perhaps over the course of a century. From the conversion to Christianity in 1000 CE until 1550 CE, Iceland was officially a Roman Catholic country, though the old gods were certainly remembered even if no longer actively worshipped. Although magic was proscribed by the Roman Catholic Church, the proscription does not appear to have been enforced with any great vigour, the authorities being more concerned with blasphemy and heresy than with the practice of magic itself. There was a dramatic reversal of attitude after Lutheran Protestantism was imposed by the Danish rulers and the fashion for witchcraft persecution was imported from Europe; then it became positively dangerous to be found with a book of magic in one's possession, and it could bring a sentence of

---

[39] This was, at least, the early modern period for mainland Europe; things moved rather slower in Iceland and it has been commented with some justification that the Middle Ages did not end there until the arrival of the electric telegraph around 1900.

exile, flogging, mutilation or even death by burning. As elsewhere, the witch-hunt mania died down by around 1720 and, by the 19th Century, antiquarian scholars were avidly collecting and copying into notebooks as many of the old spells as they could get their hands on. That is not to say that those scholars were active magicians (though it would be nice to think it); they probably collected them for the sake of curiosity. However, we owe a debt to these collectors, for they preserved many spells contained in manuscripts now lost.

The spells in the old books of magic consisted of elements already discussed in this book: magical signs, appeals to supernatural entities, incantations and so on. It is to the magical signs and images - the *galdrastafir* and *galdramyndir* - that we will look now.

The magical signs in these old Icelandic books are intriguing and often quite beautiful. Unfortunately, they are also exceedingly frustrating, being - as Sir Winston Churchill once said of Russia - "a riddle, wrapped in a mystery, inside an enigma". There are many reasons for this. Firstly, very different staves are often prescribed in separate spells for exactly the same purpose, while identical staves are sometimes used for very different purposes. Secondly, the staves frequently incorporate recurring forms and motifs, but stubbornly defy all attempts to interpret the meaning of these forms and motifs, precisely because they are so varied. Thirdly, it is quite likely that magical signs and images were shared, copied and even acquired from foreign manuscripts with little or no understanding of their significance; they were attractive, they looked powerful, so someone thought "I'll use that one!" and copied it down - complete with transcription errors and ink blots and spatters - while attaching their own meaning and intention[40]. Finally, readers already experienced

---

40 The iconoclastic Mr Eirik Storesund has written an amusingly scathing article on the confusion among modern Heathens when it comes the early modern galdrastafir and Viking-age iconography. You can find the article in full on the internet at https://www.brutenorse.com/blog/2018/5/14/the-gishjalmur

in sigil magic will know that the purpose of crafting a sigil is to create a sign that cannot be interpreted by others and, after a time, *may not even be interpreted by the conscious mind of its owner.*

So, given this frustrating situation, what are we to do as modern, practising magicians? We could, of course, simply give up and leave the study of magical staves to the dusty realm of academia, but I doubt such a solution will appeal to the questing minds of readers of this book. We could also confine ourselves to performing the spells in the old grimoires; there are, after all, many of them, though the relevance of some to modern preoccupations and environments is far to seek, and their feasibility is often dubious. For your benefit, I have included 32 of these original spells in an appendix, selected according to relevance, assumed feasibility, and the incorporation of a magical sign. A third option - my preferred one - is to forge ahead and invent a new system that will allow us to recreate sigils which have the 'look and feel' of the early modern galdrastafir. In order to create such a system, we have to evolve a 'grammar' which is firmly based upon the features we can observe among the Icelandic galdrastafir. These features are numerous and varied, so we will have to confine ourselves to a selection.

As a beginning, we can consider the option of creating bindrunes that outwardly resemble galdrastafir. This method has some problems, but also some opportunities. To remain true to the early modern period, we must discard the option of using the Elder Futhark runes, as these had been out of use for nearly a thousand years. Instead, we must rely on the rune-forms which were authentically used in the sixteenth, seventeenth and eighteenth centuries (see Chapter 3 and Appendix 2). By around 800 CE, the 24-character Elder Futhark had been replaced in the Scandinavian sphere by the 16-character Younger Futhark, with the disappearance of the esoteric lore contained in the discarded eight characters or its merging into the remaining ones.

TABLE 1: THE YOUNGER FUTHARK

Rune	Rune name	Phonetic value	Rune number
ᚠ	fé	f	1
ᚢ	úr	u	2
ᚦ	þurs	th	3
ᚭ	áss	o	4
ᚱ	reið	r	5
ᚴ	kaun	k	6
ᚼ	hagall	h	7
ᚾ	nauð	n	8
ᛁ	íss	i	9
ᛅ	ár	a	10
ᛋ	sól	s	11
ᛏ	Týr	t	12
ᛒ	bjarkan	b	13
ᛘ	maður	m	14
ᛚ	lögr	l	15
ᛦ	ýr	terminal -R	16

The text of the Old Icelandic Rune Poem, together with the kennings ascribed to the runes in other sources, indicate that some of the lore of the Elder Futhark was preserved, and sometimes altered or added to, in the shorter Younger Futhark. As a simple means of written communication, however, it had its shortcomings, because some sounds had to share the same rune: thus 'k' and 'g' were both represented by *kaun*, 'i' and 'e' were both represented by *íss*, 't' and 'd' were both represented by *Týr*, and 'b' and 'p' were both represented by *bjarkan*. The row was therefore extended again later, using modifiers in the form of dots or bars, to more closely match the Roman alphabet as shown below.

TABLE 2: THE LATER, EXTENDED ICELANDIC FUTHARK

ᛅ ᛒ ᛏ ᚦ ᚠ ᚠ ᚼ ᛁ ᚴ ᛚ ᛘ ᚾ ᚭ ᛒ ᚱ ᛋ ᛏ ᚢ ᚦ ᚯ

a/á/æ b d e f g h i/j/y k l m n o p r s t u/v þ/ð ö

Note that the runes for d, e, g and p were newly re-invented, and we cannot ascribe to them the esoteric lore of their equivalents in the Elder Futhark. They can, however, be used to create sigils which are based on written words.

Now let us take an example of how a galdrastafur-like sigil might be created to invoke the mighty name of Óðinn (Odin). We need the runes ᚭ, Þ, I and ᚠ (or ᚵ). Joined together as a bindrune, these may appear as follows:

We can then mirror the ᚭ, and Þ runes for greater symmetry, and use a long-twig ᚵ instead of the short-twig ᚠ (simply mirroring the latter would add an ᚭ (ár), which we don't want). The result so far is close to the desired image.

Finally, we can render the 'twigs' in a more rounded, cursive style, and turn the entire sigil on its side to achieve a magical stave in the Icelandic style:

The Younger Futhark and the later, extended Futhark are only two of the options available for the formation of bindrunes. It would appear that Icelandic sorcerers were not shy about inventing their own rune-rows, and many such rows are available to us, collected in (among others) Geir Vigfússon's 'Huld' manuscript (1860), the 'Rún' manuscript (1928), and in 'Galdraskræða' published by Jochum Eggertsson in 1940 under the pen-name 'Skuggi'. Some of these rows lend themselves as well - if not better - to the formation of bindrunes that can either stand alone or be incorporated into a more extensive, galdrastafur-style sigil. It is impossible to reproduce all of these rows here, but a sample from the 'Huld' manuscript is depicted below. The reader is encouraged to experiment with these rows and others, which may be found on the internet at www.handrit.is, the online manuscript section of the Icelandic National Library.

PAGE 29 OF THE 'HULD' MANUSCRIPT (NOTE THAT THE ROMAN EQUIVALENTS, IN THE ICELANDIC ALPHABETIC ORDER[41], ARE GIVEN NEAR THE TOP OF THE PAGE)

Another way in which we might incorporate one or more runes into a galdrastafur-style sigil is to use the pentimal number system, which was employed on Scandinavian clog almanacs in the modern and early modern periods. This form of numerical notation is similar in concept to Roman numerals and employs vertical staves adorned with horizontal bars and semi-circles as shown below.

---

[41] The Icelandic alphabet (at least in the case of the Huld MS) runs as follows: a, b, c, d, e, f, g, h, i, k, l, m, n, o, p, r, s, t, u, v, þ, æ, ö. Another letter, ð (a soft 'th' as in 'the') is also used but never at the beginning of words; for runic purposes it should be represented by the þ character, which is normally a hard 'th' as in 'thing'.

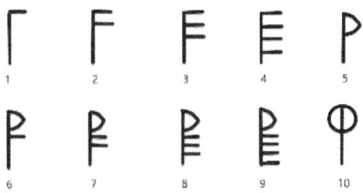

THE PENTIMAL NUMBER SYSTEM

Thus, instead of using an actual character from the Younger Futhark, one can use its numeric equivalent (see Table 1 above). The 16th rune, 'Ýr', will require a fairly long vertical shaft together with a circle (as in the pentimal number 10) plus another semi-circle and 1 horizontal bar. This is a rather good method for hiding runes within a sigil.

Creating bindrunes which resemble galdrastafir is only a beginning, and only one possible method. The authentic and original galdrastafir employed other shapes and motifs that cannot be taken to represent runes, and must have indicated some other mode of representation. Other authors such as Dr Stephen E. Flowers (a.k.a. Edred Thorsson), Greg Crowfoot and Justin Foster have already ventured to provide explanations for these shapes and motifs, and we can take their views into consideration even if we do not necessarily agree with them.

A very common form among the Icelandic magical staves is the symmetrical spoked 'wheel' typified by the Helm of Awe (Ægishjálmur) and the Vegvísir (signpost), in which four, six or eight spokes radiate from a central point. In his books 'Northern Magic' (1992) and 'Icelandic Magic' (2016), Dr Flowers considers these as maps of the magical universe, having three fields or zones: a central core, in which stands the operative magician himself or herself (or alternatively the object or aim of the magic); an outer ring representing the subjective universe of the magician; and the outside representing the objective universe.

HELM OF AWE

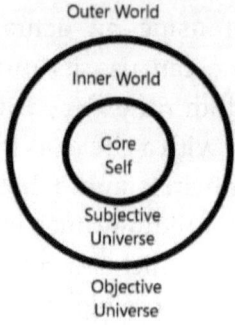

FLOWERS' 3 ZONES

I think this is a valid way of looking at the structure of such radial galdrastafir. The same might be applied to those in which we see concentric rectangles, such as in this rather complex magical image from the 'Huld' manuscript:

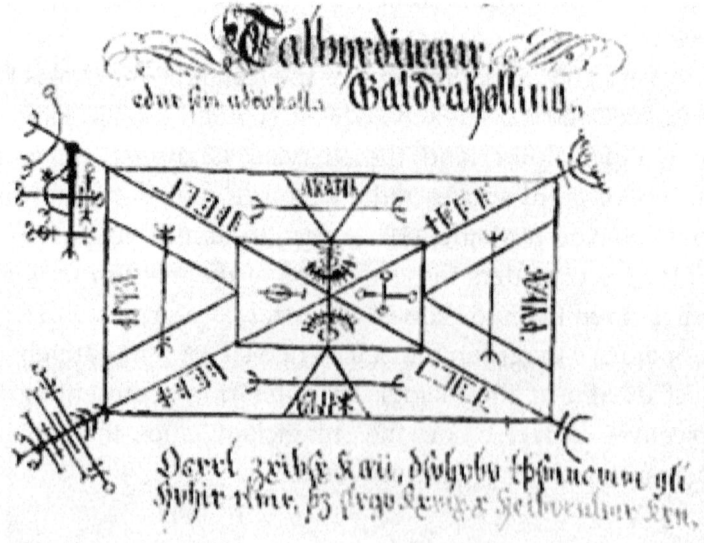

It is not the only interpretation, however. The fields or zones could also represent physical distance between the sender and the target of the magic, or the middle zone might be used to express conditions which must be fulfilled for the magic to have its effect on the ultimate target - or to prevent undesired repercussions.

As already stated, radial galdrastafir frequently have four or eight 'spokes' radiating from the centre or from a circle at the centre (though some have more than eight). These may be used to represent the four cardinal points of the compass - thus everything around one on the physical plane - and also the secondary, ordinal directions (northeast, southeast etc.) if one desires geographical precision. The eight-spoked symbols can also be a simplified representation of the nine worlds, with Midgard at the centre and surrounded by the eight outer worlds of Asgard, Vanaheim, Liosalfheim, Svartalfheim, Jotunheim, Muspelsheim, Niflheim and Hel. This representation of Yggdrasil, the World Tree, can also be embodied in snowflake-shaped, six-spoked staves as depicted below. Note that this is a three-dimensional image projected onto a flat plane: one should view the axis from Asgard to Hel as a vertical column, with the worlds of Vanaheim, Jotunheim, Muspelsheim and Niflheim at right-angles to the column and sharing the horizontal plane.

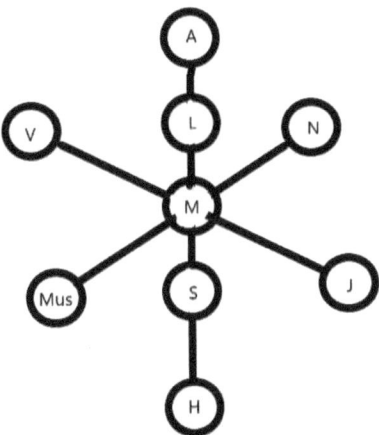

THE SIX-SPOKED, SNOWFLAKE-SHAPED STAVE AS YGGDRASIL

I find this projection[42] extremely useful, as it has clear 'up' and 'down' directions as well as the cardinal points, depicting a column of consciousness intersecting a phenomenal plane of expansive and contractive forces, organic growth, and the force of chaos and destruction. Six-spoked staves are admittedly much rarer in the old books of magic than four- or eight-spoked staves, but that is no reason not to use them when creating one's own sigils. There are, of course, many other basic forms that galdrastafir can take, including squares, triangles, an upright or inverted 'V' and simple linear forms, and I refer you to Appendix 5 for some of these. The magician must choose for himself which basic shape is appropriate for his intention. It is also possible to use ideograms for the basic shape, such as a simplified house, a matchstick man, or a bird in flight.

Stave Terminations

Icelandic magical staves are also strongly characterised by the terminations of their lines or spokes, and also the signs to be found at their beginning and halfway along the line. They can consist of rounded or squared forks, T-terminations, X-terminations, circle terminations and beginnings, rounded terminations, horizontal bars, inward and outward-facing curves, and so on. It seems apparent that these motifs must once have formed a complex magical grammar, but now we can only guess at their meanings. At least three people - Dr Stephen Flowers, Greg Crowfoot and Justin Foster - have attempted to interpret these signs in recent years, and their interpretations are summarised in the table below.

---

[42] Those of you who have read 'Runelore' by Edred Thorsson (see bibliography) will recognise this projection, and I think it an elegant and beautiful illustration of the structure of Yggdrasil. I have omitted the secondary ways between the worlds here for the sake of clarity.

Working Name	Image	Flowers	Crowfoot	Foster
Trident		Traps power and prevents it returning to its source	Acts in more profound manner (than straight trident) to prevent return flow	
Squared Trident		Catches and holds power	Radiates energy and prevents return flow	Captures and collects energy
Outward-facing curve			Catches returning energy and prevents it reaching the wearer	Allows energy in and blocks energy from flowing back out
Inward-facing curve				Energy can flow out and is blocked from coming in
T-termination		Prevents power from diffusing	Prevents diffusion of magical energy	Keeps energy concentrated, undiffuse and undiluted
Circle termination		Returns power to the source	Recirculates some of energy of Helm back into itself, recharging it automatically	Returns energy back to its owner

Straight Trident	—<	Dynamizes and activates power	Acts as activator, radiating power of Helm outwards into space	Activates and radiates energy
Bars	—|||—		Accelerates or amplifies energy invoked by sigil as a whole	Amplifies or charges energy as it travels through

Dr Flowers' interpretations were given in 'Northern Magic' (1992), written under his pen name Edred Thorsson. In his later work 'Icelandic Magic' (2016), he does not return to the subject of stave terminations at all, and may have thought it better to let readers ascribe their own meanings based on what they perceive in the old staves. In the former work, he concludes the section on Helm of Awe-type sigils by saying:

> *"With this kind of sign, as well as with others with no objective way to 'read' their meanings, the vocally performed incantation or prayer is of great importance. It makes clear what the will of the magician is and puts the final precise 'polish' to the spell. For the helm to work properly it is, as always, of the utmost importance that magicians themselves be sure, in no uncertain terms, as to what their intentions are."*

In "Understanding the Galdrabók & Creating Original Designs"[43], Greg Crowfoot takes Flowers' interpretations of the motifs and adds a couple of his own, namely the outward-facing curve and the three perpendicular bars which are frequently to be seen in the middle of lines or spokes. As a guide to creating one's original sigil designs, the book is

---

43 I have searched for a print copy of this work, and would have been prepared to pay for it, but it only seems to be available in the form of bootleg digital copies on the internet. I found my copy at scribd.com,

useful, but unfortunately rather spoiled by his consistent use of the Elder Futhark which, as already noted, had been out of vogue for about a thousand years by the time the manuscript which Flowers calls 'The Galdrabók' was compiled. It is therefore no guide to understanding that book of magic, nor to creating galdrastafur designs that are anything like authentic.

Justin Foster, a researcher based in Australia, has a very useful website at www.galdrastafir.com. On this website, he provides a table of stave motifs and terminations based on readings of Flowers and Crowfoot, but also adding what I have designated the 'inward-facing curve'. He adds: "Whilst these theories about energy flows seem plausible, I tend to favour my own or other theories. I believe the inward and outward facing cups are to invoke God or gods. I am also quite confident that a circle usually represents a person or people, with a centre circle being the self." I consider this a valid approach, and concur that the circle motif - whether at the centre of a radial stave or as terminations - can represent a person or persons.

My System

Taking all the above into consideration, and discarding some of it, I developed my own system of stave motifs, and I will elaborate on this now. Do please note that this is an entirely new system! It is inspired by the original galdrastafir, but it is not intended as a guide to understanding them.

1. Curved and straight tridents

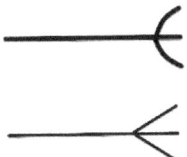

I consider both versions of this trident termination as essentially the same, the straight-armed version lending itself better to carving on wood or metal. The trident motif is the most common termination among the ancient galdrastafir. It is an assertive, outward emission of magical power, firmly imposing the will of the magician on the objective universe.

2. Squared trident

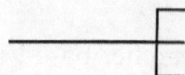

A variant of the curved and straight tridents, this aggressively sends out power and then fixes the result, resisting attempts by external forces to change it.

3. Shield

This termination shields the magician from external forces, and is therefore good for warding spells.

4. T-termination

This termination, as its form suggests, puts a stop to ongoing matters and firmly signals "This is ended!"

5. Circle start (or centre)

This represents the magician him/herself, or the beneficiary (e.g. a person, house or pet) of a spell - often as a talisman.

6. Circle termination

A circle termination at the outer end of a radial spoke or of a line (depending on the direction in which the spell is to be read in linear staves) stands for persons or things - usually specified - which are the target of the magic.

7. Outward-facing curve in centre of line or spoke

In the middle of a line or spoke, this energises and augments the effect of the ultimate termination.

8. Inward-facing curve in centre of line or spoke

This helps to shield the sender from the consequences of the stave termination and prevents a backflow of energy. It can also be used to augment the effect of a shielding termination (see number 3 above).

9. Bars perpendicular to the line or spoke

Bars like these can be used either to represent a rune by its number according to the pentimal system, or they can represent stages in the narrative of the stave, as dictated by the sender. Their meaning in the latter case is entirely subjective and known only to the sender.

10. X-termination

This termination, inspired by a number of old thief-finding staves, represents searching for knowledge and bringing it back to the magician.

These motifs can be combined in almost endless permutations as outward expressions of the magician's will. Better still, they can be added to a rune-based sigil in order to heighten or specify its effect.

Galdramyndir

'Mynd' in Icelandic means a picture or image, so a galdramynd (pl. galdramyndir) is a magical picture or image. These work on exactly the same basis as galdrastafir, but are more elaborate, presenting a broader canvas on which to 'paint' your intention. As they require quite a lot of work, they are best employed for talismans which are expected to function for a long time rather than for short-term measures. Once again, the basic shape is a matter of choice and expediency.

Perhaps the best way to explain their construction is to give a detailed account of how I developed one to counter the Covid-19 virus when it first made its appearance in the United Kingdom. The intention of the magical operation was to contain and kill the virus. At that stage, one of the few things we knew about it was that it was vulnerable to heat, so killing it with fire seemed appropriate. Firstly, I needed a sigil with which to represent the virus itself. I composed a bindrune using the later, extended Futhark characters for 'kofid' and the ancillary rune *belgþor* (Φ) which was used on Scandinavian clog almanacs to represent the number 19. This was then surrounded and contained by a double lozenge with enough space between the two lozenges to allow room for writing the summarised intention in Icelandic: *"Setjið skepnuna í búr.*

Drepið hana með eldi" (Cage the beast. Kill it with fire). Finally, the corners of the double lozenge were given extensions with *nauð* runes (to bind) and *þurs* runes (to smash). The result is depicted below.

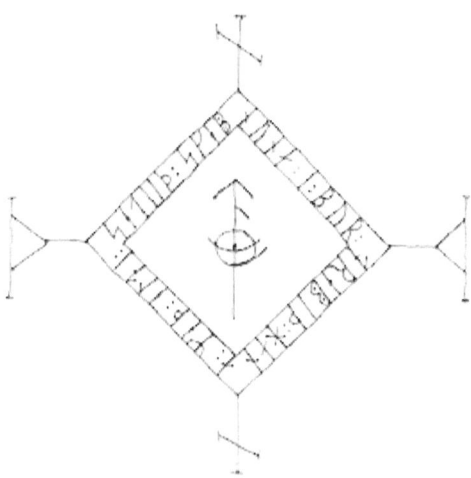

It is not a very complex magical image compared to some which can be found in the old books of magic, but in this case the intention was to burn it after performing an incantation.

CHAPTER 11

THE METHODS OF DELIVERY

Even in the planning stage of your magical operation, you will need to give thought to the method by which your spell is to be delivered to the target. The considerations are entirely practical, and depend on the nature of your target and your degree of access to the same.

Talismanic Magic

Talismans and amulets are frequently taken to be the same thing, so it is useful to maintain a distinction. A talisman is an object that bears some kind of sign and/or inscription that endows it with magic, whereas an amulet is a magical object that bears no sign or inscription, but is considered to be magical in its own right. Examples of amulets are gems that are held to be endowed with specific properties, a 'lucky rabbit's foot', or a horseshoe. Here we will only consider talismans. A talisman is usually prepared and given its 'doom', or purpose, in a rite within the confines of one's own stead. After that, they are hung on, or otherwise affixed to, the person, animal or object forming the target of the magic. This naturally assumes a large degree of acquiescence and compliance on the part of the target, so this method is most useful in spells intended to benefit yourself, your property, or those you love. Typically, these will be apotropaic spells (to ward you against evil or general misfortune), healing spells, or spells to bring luck. You can hang a talisman around your neck, keep it in your purse or wallet, hang it on your pet's collar, or place it by the threshold of your home. Unless it was designed and named for a specific target, a talisman can also be transferable. Talismans are perhaps the most useful items in your inventory of spells. They are often long-lasting, and can be valuable repositories of stored power. After all, nobody can expect to be at the top of their game at all times; no matter how well we try to keep ourselves on top form, life can sometimes wear us down and force us to fall back on friends and allies (see also Chapter 7). A talisman, well crafted, can be such an ally in time of need. It can take the form of a medallion, a walking stick, a wand, a piece of parchment, or a ring. When giving a talisman its mission, you can also programme it to respond in certain ways under certain circumstances. A general-purpose talisman, such as one for luck and/or protection, can be recharged when you are feeling particularly buoyant, joyful and powerful (as after a successful working) by wilfully directing some of that power into it. Programming of this type is very useful if there is any chance that others might touch the talisman. In general, you should not allow other people to touch your magical objects without your permission, but sometimes it is unavoidable, as I realised once when an airport security officer had her interfering hands all over my bag of rune-lots and its contents. In anticipation of such an event happening again, I programmed my walking stick to draw in energy from others when they touch it without my express permission, and to emit an unpleasant sensation as if they were handling thorns. This appears to work, and a fellow magician commented on it even when he touched the stick with my permission.

Direct Carving

'Carving', as already mentioned, does not necessarily refer to literal carving (though sometimes it does); in this context, it can also mean writing a sign or simply tracing it in blood or spittle. Some old Icelandic spells for the protection or healing of livestock also use the term when they actually mean that a stave should be clipped into the wool, fur or hair of the animal in question. Direct carving is best used when you wish to transfer a magical intention to an existing person (including yourself), an animal or an object. It can be used to charm tools and weapons to make them more effective. This is well attested in the 'Lay of Sigrdrifa' (part of the Poetic Edda), in which the Valkyrie Sigrdifa enjoins the hero Sigurd:

> *"Learn victory runes if thou victory wantest,*
> *and have them on thy sword's hilt -*
> *on thy sword's hilt some, on thy sword's guard some,*
> *and call twice upon Týr.*[44]*"*

Two traditional Icelandic spells can be found in Appendix 5, one for charming the sinker of one's fishing line in order to catch more fish, and another for charming a whetstone so that it will sharpen tools better. Runes and staves can also be directly carved on objects you own, such as the doorpost of your home or a casket that you wish to hide from prying eyes. You can also 'carve' magical staves onto your skin using a finger (the ring finger of either hand appears to have been favoured) wetted with your own spittle in a deed of 'instant' magic. Such a method is excellent when one has no time to plan in advance, and you simply wish to get something done right now without the requirement for a lasting result in the long term. I was once at an airport with my family, queuing to check in for a flight. The queue seemed endless, and didn't appear to be moving much, so I went into a meditative trance, focusing on Fehu (for quickening) and Raiðo (to represent the queue, the path we needed to take). After a few deep breaths to absorb the runic might and awaken it in myself, I traced a sigil binding the two runes with spittle on the palm of my left hand, then blew across the palm to send it to the queue ahead of us. Almost at once, the queue began to move and we were soon at the check-in desk. On another occasion, I was getting rather fed up of losing to a friend at a card-driven skirmish wargame, so I traced an Icelandic stave for winning in card games on my palm with spittle, and secured a resounding victory.

---

[44] Translation by Lee M. Hollander.

Delivery by Transference

This involves bringing an already prepared spell into direct contact with the target. This method is frequently advocated in the old grimoires for spells intended to change your relationship with a targeted person, generally to gain the love or friendship of that person. The spell is prepared in advance on paper, vellum or a slip of wood, or it may be traced on one's palm (see 'Direct Carving' above). You then have to get the person to accept the spell, or secrete it in their clothing, or (if you have traced the stave on your palm) simply shake hands with them. These days, you could also send it by post (17th-century Iceland had no postal service). Those familiar with the writings of M.R. James will recognise it as the method used in his story 'Casting the Runes'. As in this story, there is always a danger that the recipient may find a way to return the spell to the sender. Because of the element of subterfuge and breach of trust, delivery by transference is frequently used for spells with malign intent. Another, very similar, method is delivery by ingestion. Here, the spell is cast on some food or beverage, which is then given to a person to eat or drink. Ingestion is also a historically attested method to learn the inner lore of the runes: bake small cakes or biscuits (cookies) with a rune marked on each of them, then eat one and meditate on the rune in question. Alternatively, you can eat it before going to sleep and see what is revealed in your dreams.

Delivery by Proximity

All the aforementioned methods involve direct contact with the target, but, in some cases, it is enough to merely place a stave, rune or bindrune near its target. Historically, love charms were covertly scratched on the bed of the object of one's desire, or hidden under the mattress. Curse-tablets might be buried next to the threshold of the victim's house, or a spell could otherwise be concealed along a path that the target could be expected to take. Many of the traditional

Icelandic spells specify that such operations should be performed secretly, leaving the victim 'unknowing' (*óvitandi*), but occasionally they were meant to be done overtly, as with the 'Terror Stave' (*óttastafur*) that was to be carved on a piece of oak and cast before an enemy's feet in order to terrify him.

TERROR STAVE FROM THE HULD MANUSCRIPT

Unlike direct carving and transference, delivery by proximity does not necessarily require close access to the target, but it does call for access to the place where the target is or will be located - usually the longer the better.

Delivery from a Distance

This method calls for more skill and confidence in your ability, but it pays dividends to master it because you can then project your will wherever you wish, regardless of distance. In the old, traditional spells, this was sometimes done using an incantation alone, and sometimes with a stave (or staves) alone, but more often with a combination of both. This is where the art of projecting the runes - signing and sending (see Chapter 4) - comes into play. If you can clearly visualise your target, and know its rough direction, then you can send your magical intention straight to it. If you have difficulty doing that, you can also use an image (perhaps a photograph) of your target to focus on. Signing and sending across distances requires a lot of practice and good visualisation, but it can be devastatingly effective. While we were still getting to know each other, my wife and I communicated daily via Skype. At the time, she had an unwanted guest in her household, who had been injudiciously referred to her as a homeless military veteran temporarily in need of a couch to crash on. Regrettably, he turned out to be a boorish oaf who lay on the couch all day watching TV, evaded requests to leave, and became undesirably familiar. I had never seen the house, nor had I seen the man in question, but the emotional link with the woman who would one day be my wife probably proved sufficient. I said "Wait a minute", and suddenly went into a light trance. Using the runes Thurisaz and Isa, I visualised enormous, foot-long thorns sprouting from the couch, while the room froze until hoar frost spread, crackling, all over the walls. Then I came back to the present and my wife asked "What just happened there?" I replied, with absolute confidence, "He will be gone within three days." And he was. Afterwards, my wife asked her mother if she had noticed anything unusual about the man's behaviour just prior to his departure. "Why yes", she replied, "he kept getting up from the couch as if he couldn't get comfortable. He started wearing his coat indoors and turning the heating up all the time." The distance between us had been nearly 5,000 miles as the crow flies.

When to deliver?

If you have prepared a magical object in a ritual setting, you will have to perform the closing rite first before delivering it to its target. This holds true even if the magical object is a talisman for your own use, and you have only to hang it around your neck. Spells that are to be delivered by transference, plus some others involving tracing with finger and spittle, generally fall into the 'instant magic' category and do not call for an elaborate ritual. They are delivered as and when necessary. or as soon as is convenient.

CHAPTER 12

TIME AND SPACE

Let us sum up what you have learned so far. You know how to enter into a trance state by breathing regularly and emptying your mind. You have a basic knowledge of the runes, their meanings and their forms and phonemes. You know how to carve and colour the runes, and how to sign and send them. You have everything you need to create a ritual act of magic, consisting of:

- The opening;
- Evocation of the appropriate deity or deities;
- Composing and performing an incantation;
- Carving a symbol embodying your intention in the form of one or more runes (which may be combined to create a bindrune) or a magical stave (*galdrastafur*);
- Delivering your magical spell to its target (though this may come after the closing);
- The closing of the rite.

You know what to do, but when is it to be done? And where? Is there any time or place that is more propitious than another? In many cases, the answer will clearly resound "Here and now!", for we cannot always predict when we might need to use magic to get out of a sticky situation. For what use would magic be, if we cannot bring it up precisely when we need it? Then there are the small acts of magic which we should perform daily, such as warding our home or bringing protection before embarking on a journey. Fortunately, however, we frequently have time to plan ahead in order to create a spell of enduring effect or one that is to take effect at a time and place of our choosing.

TIME

The timing of northern magic is primarily governed by the daily, monthly and annual cycles of the Sun and Moon. If the ancient Germanic tribes ever developed any system of astrology similar to the one commonly known today (which originated in the Near East), then this has been all but lost to us, though we do know of some northern names for certain stars and constellations. It is quite possible that no such system was developed; the climates of north-western Europe and of Iceland make for cloudy skies and are less conducive to speculation on the movements of the stars and planets. This is not to say that you cannot incorporate modern astrology into your own magical practice, only that it would appear to have been less used in the practical magic of the north. The Icelandic books of magic sometimes give instructions that spells are to be performed at a certain time of day or at a specific point in the lunar cycle. Sunrise[45] and noon appear to have been regarded as propitious times, together with the third, sixth or ninth days after the New Moon, plus Full Moon. Only one annual feast is mentioned as magically significant, and that is the Eve of St John's Mass (Old Midsummer's Eve, the 23rd of June); however, this only reflects a small sample of six Icelandic grimoires, and magical or divinatory rites were (and still are) certainly performed at other times of year in the Germanic world[46]. The study of feast-days, folklore and local customs is a vast subject, and one that will reward study. Here, however, I must confine myself to some general observations based on practical experience.

---

[45] The actual words given are "When the sun is in the east". One must remember that in Iceland - due to its high latitude - the points of sunrise and sunset vary wildly throughout the year. At midwinter, the sun barely raises her head above the horizon, while at midsummer she barely sets.

[46] An example is the Swedish Årsgång (year walk) custom, a night-time walk to the churchyard, taken alone, in silence and while fasting, in order to gain knowledge of the year's coming events. It is performed on New Year's Eve.

As previously mentioned, the daily, monthly and annual cycles of the sun and moon should be taken into account when planning your rites, and we will discuss these under the simple headings of 'Daily', 'Monthly' and 'Seasonal'.

Daily

Every day, the Sun rises, climbs to her zenith, then takes the descending journey to her point of setting. All of nature moves with her, and it pays the magician also to attune him- or herself to the daily cycle. Magical workings oriented towards inception - starting something - are best performed at sunrise, while workings designed to bring something to full manifestation should be performed when the sun is at her zenith. The time around sunset and dusk can best be used for spells designed to rid yourself of something (an undesirable habit, for example) or to enhance quiet contemplation and fulfilment. The hours of darkness (especially at midnight) are a good time for malign magic, curses, divination and gaining knowledge of hidden things. You can also enhance your working by performing it on an appropriate day of the week. This is not really a traditional part of Germanic magic, but it pays to be eclectic. The seven-day Roman week was adopted by the Germanic peoples at some time between the fourth and sixth centuries CE, and most of the Roman day names were interpreted in terms of their familiar deities. A table of the days and their attributions is shown below.

DAYS OF THE WEEK

Roman Name	Modern English Name	Deity/Body	Some Attributes
Dies Solis	Sunday	Sun	Guidance; victory; good for all benign workings.
Dies Lunae	Monday	Moon	Divination; calling upon ancestors.
Dies Martis	Tuesday	Tiw/Týr	War & strife; justice; courage; self-discipline.
Dies Mercurii	Wednesday	Woden/Odin	Inspiration; poetry; guile; commerce; good for all magic.
Dies Jovis	Thursday	Thunor/Thor	Physical strength; breaking down barriers; weather magic; healing.
Dies Veneris	Friday	Freya	Fertility; organic growth; general prosperity.
Dies Saturni	Saturday	Saturn*	Stability; impeding enemies; contemplation.

*Note that Saturn is not a Germanic deity, and it appears that no satisfactory comparative deity could be found in the Germanic pantheon. In the Scandinavian countries, Saturday was 'laugardagr' or 'bath day'.

Monthly

As the word implies, monthly cycles are governed by the Moon. In Germanic mythology, the Moon is male and his sister, the Sun, is female[47]. The Moon waxes and wanes over a cycle lasting approximately 29 days, from New Moon, when the Moon is not visible, to Full Moon and back again, and his movements and phases have magical significance in every culture on earth. As with the daily cycle of the Sun, the monthly phases of the Moon can be auspicious for broadly different magical intentions. The start of the waxing period, when the Moon shows in the sky as a thin crescent just after sunset, is good for new ventures. It is a good idea to keep an eye out for this phase - try to see the Moon for the first time in each new cycle without looking through glass; bow 3 times towards him, and 'turn your money over' (i.e. rotate your purse or wallet) for good luck and prosperity. If cloudy skies prevail, this phase may be missed altogether, and you should consider the opportunity passed if the Moon has already reached First Quarter by the time you see him. The entire waxing phase is good for operations of growth and positivity. The time of the Full Moon is considered auspicious for rites intended to bring manifestation and fulfilment, and also for divination. For best results, choose the night before complete fullness. The waning phases of the Moon are good for operations designed to diminish or rid yourself of something, and to break fetters of various kinds. In general, no magic should be performed during the three days around the time of the New Moon, but this is a good time for reflection and for making plans.

Seasonal

In pre-industrial society, life was governed by the seasons, and this was reflected in seasonal rites and feasts. Though there were few times when agricultural activity ceased altogether; some periods were relatively relaxed while others were quite hectic. After the mid-winter festivities, when no work at all was to be done, the ground had to be

---

[47] To be more accurate, Moon (Máni) and Sun (Sunna or Sól) are the beings who were appointed by the gods to ride their respective heavenly bodies across the sky.

prepared by plough and harrow (the frost also helping to break up the clods). Then came the sowing, followed by the growth and ripening of various crops. The lambing season was also a busy time, and the growth of new, lush grass in spring was a bonus for livestock. May was known to the Anglo-Saxons as *Thrimilce*, the month when cattle could be milked three times per day. The summer month of June was a relatively fallow one, but crops still had to be laboriously weeded. It was also a prime month for war. In late July, the harvest began - first the hay, and then the cereal crops - and the first harvest feast was celebrated at Lammas, or August Eve. August was the busiest month of all, when every available hand bore scythes or sickles to bring in the grain harvest, often starting at first light and not finishing until after sunset. Ever wondered why schoolchildren get a long holiday from late July until the beginning of September? It was a concession to farmers and their labourers, who needed the help of the children to bring in the crops. Then there was the threshing, storage and milling, plus the gathering of autumn nuts and berries. Pigs were herded into woodland to fatten on acorns and beech-mast in October. November was known as 'Blood Month', for then surplus livestock was slaughtered to ease the problem of feeding it through the coming winter. Nothing went to waste. Finally came the dark, sleepy days of December, and the completion of the annual cycle was celebrated again with feasting.

How different are our lives today, when only a small percentage of us work on the land, the majority having only the vaguest idea of where their food comes from, or the work which brought it to the table! We work for most of the year in factories or offices, isolated from the elements, sometimes getting a short but begrudged break on public holidays that no longer bear any relationship to our working lives. Then, in August, which used to be a time of frantic activity, we stop working and head off for a couple of weeks of lazing in the sun.

It rewards the modern magician to re-acquire an awareness of the annual cycle of nature, for this will greatly benefit his or her magic when planning it over the longer term. This does not mean that you need to give up your job and live a primitive, back-to-nature existence, but you can go some way towards it by simply being observant and giving thought to the changing of the seasons. Consciously watch how the days lengthen and shorten. Walk regularly in your local park and note how green nature evolves over the year: waxing, blossoming, seeding, and dying, eventually to wax again. Attune your plans to the wheel of the year:

Winter - a time to plan and contemplate;

Spring - a time to prepare the ground and plant those spells that are to bear fruit later;

Summer - a time to execute plans, to weed out what opposes you and, if necessary, to make war;

Autumn - a time to harvest and ensure that the deeds laid down earlier bear fruit.

And, in all seasons, make an effort to keep a feast that is meaningful to you. It can be a traditional feast, or one of your own invention, but be sure to raise a glass or horn to yourself in celebration of the effort you have put in!

SPACE AND DIRECTION

Some of the spells in the old Icelandic grimoires offer clear instructions regarding the location in which they are to be performed and/or the direction one is to face or to move. Regrettably, such spells are so few that it is hard to draw any firm or useful conclusions from them, and one must fall back on other, long-established lore. Just as the Icelandic sorcerers of old may have mainly operated within their isolated, turf-built houses, your main magical space will be the *stead* that you establish in your home. Here you will usually have the best guarantee of the privacy you require for your rites. Granted, not everyone is blessed with an understanding family and considerate neighbours and, if you cannot find the quiet seclusion that you need, then you may have to find a different place or adapt your timetable so that you work your magic when everyone else is away or asleep. In such restricted situations, you can draw some comfort from the fact that, with good visualisation skills, magic can be done within the confines of your own imagination. After all, it is from the heart and mind that the real business of sorcery is done; all the rest - the altar, candles, incense and tools - are mere trappings, simple aids to assist you in manifesting a narrative that is conceived on an ideal plane that is not physical. Consider this: you read my words at this moment, absorbing their meaning, learning from them and perhaps forming an image of the author as he writes; but the concepts were conceived in my mind before they were formulated into words, and the words were typed on an electronic medium before they came to be printed. Is this not quite magical in itself?

However, let us for the present assume that you have the benefit of a personal stead where you can find the necessary solitude. Spatial matters then largely come down to direction, which we shall deal with in a moment. On occasion, though, you may feel the need to venture out into the countryside and the wilder places to take advantage of their associations and the presence of their resident wights. You may not have to go far, as even major cities often have extensive green spaces, but for a really fulfilling experience it is best to get out along the path less trodden. Certain features will immediately recommend themselves for your purpose. There will be times when you wish to ground yourself, find your inner core again, and spend time in contemplation. Earth-oriented locations such as caves and ancient standing stones are excellent for this. At other times, you may wish to reflect on the connection between heaven and earth, or perform a rite involving Tiw (Týr), in which case a high place such as the summit of a hill or mountain is recommended. For change, intellect and inspiration, select a place where the wind can be relied upon to blow. Water courses - streams and rivers - are good places for calming oneself and reflecting on Wyrd and the twists, turns and eddies of life. Whatever the case, let instinct be your guide. Some places can feel ecstatically welcoming, while others can feel ominous and doom-laden. If you feel uncomfortable, threatened or overawed in a situation, then you must first step back from yourself and try to analyse the form of the perceived threat; it may be that you are strong enough to overcome the threat and to communicate with the wight from which the threat emanates; if not, then get out of the area quickly. But walk, don't run. Remember that malefic wights are not corporeal, and that the harm they can inflict arises only from your own panic and the likelihood of you tumbling down a rocky precipice or into a river.

Magic is always a matter of connecting different worlds. It works ever on the edge of things, the point between the vast realm of possibility and actual manifestation. On the edge, the boundary, matters can go in either direction; it might require only a nudge of the will to make them fall on one side or the other. The term we use for this is liminality, from the Latin word 'limes': a boundary or limit. We experience liminality in all kinds of ways. Sometimes there are hard borders - the door of your bedroom; the boundaries of your property; the division between your county and the next. At other times, the borders are fluid and permeable, such as the boundary between sleep and waking (or when in a meditative trance). Liminal places abound in the physical landscape, and can be exploited as locations where magical operations may get a boost. Crossroads and other path junctions have long been known as magical places, as are hedges and the stiles which cross them[48]. Shorelines and marshes are also liminal, being places where land and water mingle. A good, foggy night is also a good time and place for performing magic, for then all things tend to lose their form, and possibilities are opened.

Then we come to the matter of direction. In the northern tradition, one should honour what Nigel Pennick calls "The Primacy of the North"[49]. All things revolve around the world-axis, the *Yrminsul*, which extends from the centre of the earth to the celestial north pole, closely marked by the Pole Star. In the sky's northern quarter are things most constant, with

---

[48] The Old English word for a witch was *haegtesse*, literally a 'hedge-rider'.
[49] Pennick, Nigel "Pagan Magic of the Northern Tradition", Chapter 3. See bibliography.

constellations that never set; this is the direction in which Asgard is to be sought, insofar as we can relate the outer worlds to this physical realm of Midgard, and it is the direction one should face when addressing the Aesir. The harrow, or altar, in your stead should face this direction.

The other cardinal points also have their respective significances:

- East, the orientation of the rising sun, but also the direction from which the coldest blasts come in winter. This direction is also classically attributed in the Western Tradition to elemental Air, the most chaotic of the elements, and this elemental attribution has been widely adopted by rune-magicians. In the northern tradition, it is the quarter where the Etins (giants) reside beyond the borders of Midgard, but also where Sunna first shows her face in the endless potential of the dawn hour. It is a good quarter to address when starting something new, when seeking the wisdom of the Etins, or when throwing all to the hazard.
- South, the orientation of the mid-day sun, is of course associated with heat and elemental Fire. It is also associated with the world of Muspelsheim, one of the two primal worlds which existed even before the gods were born. From the clash of Fire and Ice in the Primal Void (Ginnungagap), all things came into existence, and it will be the fire of Muspelsheim that will sweep over this world in the end. In the meantime, we see this fire manifested in many ways in our Midgard, from the pleasant warmth of an ideal summer to the scorching, killing heat of a drought summer. Fire appeals to the heart and the passions, and this quarter is a good one to address in works directed towards lust and courage, among others.
- West, the orientation of the setting sun: for the peoples of north-western Europe, the sun was often to be seen setting into the western sea, and thus it is associated with elemental Water. The west is also frequently

thought of as the direction in which one departs after death towards the afterlife, as witnessed by the old expression "gone west" to describe someone who has died or something which has been irrecoverably lost. I personally associate the west with the Vanir and their home, Vanaheim, though there is little evidence for this in the lore of the Eddas[50]. The west is a good quarter to address in works that have a 'watery' or 'emotional' theme, works in which the Vanir are evoked, and also works to overcome grief and gain acceptance of departure.

---

[50] My association of the west with Vanaheim may be down to seeing Edred Thorsson's depiction of the structure of Yggdrasil (see "Runelore", p. 154), in which Vanaheimr is diametrically opposite Jötunheimr. However, there are other reasons to associate the Vanir with the west. The Vanic god Njörðr resides on the coast at Nóatún (ship-enclosure), which in Norway would almost always have lain in the west. There is also a short passage in the Saga of Gisli in which it is written "There was something else that seemed to have a strange meaning, that snow never stayed on the south-west side of Thorgrim's mound and it did not freeze there; and men explained this by saying that he must have been so favoured by Frey for his sacrifices that the god was unwilling to have frost come between them." ("Three Icelandic Outlaw Sagas" Viking Society for Northern Research 2004.)

CHAPTER 13

SENDINGS

A recurring theme in tales of Icelandic magic is the 'Sending'. In essence, this is a creature called into existence by one or more sorcerers and sent to perform some mission – usually a malevolent one. In some tales, this may be a *draugr*, i.e. a reanimated corpse. In the tale of Mori of Irafell, for example, a woman named Ingibjörg married a respected farmer named Kort Þorvarðsson. A number of her previously jilted suitors paid a wizard 'from the north' (probably the Westfjords) to direct a Sending against Kort and his wife. To make the Sending, "the wizard used a little boy who, so the story goes, had died of exposure in the open country. The wizard called him back while he was still warm, or even not quite dead, and sent him against Kort and his wife at Modruvellir[51]." In other tales, the wizard needs only a single bone from a human corpse in order to create the Sending. In such stories, the victim can defeat the Sending if he or she can strike it with an iron point at the exact spot where that single bone is located. Sometimes this is done by sheer luck, and sometimes because the bone's location shows as a white mark on an otherwise black spectre. The Sending might also, as in the tale of Thorgeir's Bull, take the form of a bull that was flayed to the knees and dragged its flayed hide behind it, and might be combined with the essences of other creatures to

---

51 Jacqueline Simpson, "Icelandic Folktales and Legends" p. 143

increase its power[52]. It appears that Sendings were also able to shape-shift, and might manifest themselves in a variety of ways: as a revenant from the dead, as the aforesaid flayed bull, as a spectre, a vapour, a ball of wool, a dry horse-turd, an insect, or simply an intimation that "something wicked this way comes." A russet colour is often associated with them. Sendings were often sent to perform a single mission – usually destructive - but could also be retained to serve a person for extended period – even for the sorcerer's entire life. They could also continue in existence for long after their original intended victim had passed away, continuing to harass his offspring and his neighbours. However, if frustrated in its aim by someone equally versed in the magical arts (or just plain lucky), the Sending could be labelled "Return to sender" and wreak its harm on the one who sent it!

The generation and manipulation of Sendings is one of the most useful and powerful arts that one can have at one's command. As a technique, it enables the sorcerer to create a powerful artificial entity with a well-defined mission spanning a lesser or greater length of time, depending upon the sorcerer's own power and the effort put into creating it. You do not need to reanimate a corpse, flay a bull, or even have a single bone. All you need is your own knowledge, emotion, imagination and *hamingja* (accumulated power and luck) to generate an entity that, while actively imagined, is certainly more than imaginary. It can be done surprisingly easily, and even spontaneously when we are going through a period of stress or high emotion. Dion Fortune described such an episode in her book "Psychic Self Defence" and her account is worth retelling in detail:

> "I had received serious injury from someone who, at

---

[52] The reference to a bull flayed to its knees and dragging its hide behind it may hark back to some cruel magical practice of ancient times. I once read an historical account of a British officer witnessing, during the Zulu War of 1879, several native auxiliaries of the Natal Native Contingent gathered around an exhausted ox as they cut hide from its body while it yet lived; the NNC auxiliaries wanted the hide to make shields, and they held that a shield would be more magically effective if cut from the hide of a living beast.

considerable cost to myself, I had disinterestedly helped, and I was sorely tempted to retaliate. Lying on my bed resting one afternoon, I was brooding over my resentment, and while so brooding, drifted towards the borders of sleep. There came to my mind the thought of casting off all restraint and going berserk. The ancient Nordic myths rose before me, and I thought of Fenris, the Wolf-horror of the North. Immediately I felt a curious drawing-out sensation from my solar plexus, and there materialised beside me on the bed a large wolf. It was a well-materialised ectoplasmic form... I could distinctly feel its back pressing against me as it lay beside me on the bed as a large dog might. I knew nothing about the art of making elementals at that time, but had accidentally stumbled upon the right method - the brooding highly charged with emotion, the invocation of the appropriate natural force, and the condition between sleeping and waking in which the etheric double readily extrudes. I was horrified at what I had done, and knew I was in a tight corner and that everything depended upon my keeping my head. I had had enough experience of practical occultism to know that the thing I had called into visible manifestation could be controlled by my will provided I did not panic; but that if I lost my nerve and it got the upper hand, I had a Frankenstein monster to cope with. I stirred slightly, and the creature evidently objected to being disturbed, for it turned its long snout towards me over its shoulder, and snarled, showing its teeth. I had now "got the wind" up properly; but I knew that everything depended on my getting the upper hand and keeping it, and that the best thing I could do was to fight it out now, because the longer the Thing remained in existence, the stronger it would get, and the more difficult to disintegrate. So I drove my elbow into its hairy ectoplasmic ribs and said to it out loud: "If you can't behave yourself, you will have to go on the floor," and pushed it off the bed. Down it

> *went, meek as a lamb, and changed from wolf to dog, to my great relief. Then the northern corner of the room appeared to fade away, and the creature went out through the gap. I was far from happy, however, for I had a feeling that this was not the end of it, and my feeling was confirmed when next morning another member of my household reported that her sleep had been disturbed by dreams of wolves, and she had awakened in the night to see the eye of a wild animal shining in the darkness in the corner of her room[53]."*

Though Dion Fortune described her spontaneous creation as an artificial elemental, it was in fact, to all intents and purposes, identical to an Icelandic Sending.

We generate thought-forms all the time and invest in them a greater or lesser degree of emotion. Sometimes we house these thoughts and emotions in otherwise inanimate objects; for example, who has not had a favourite doll or teddy-bear in childhood and made of it a companion that lived and even spoke to us? Thought-forms alone tend to be insubstantial, and fade away quickly if not dwelt upon, but you can consciously take it a step further and create a magical being that has a life of its own and a purpose to fulfil. In the old Icelandic folk tales, passed down to us by Jón Árnason, a Sending is almost always a malign wight bent on death or causing misery; such things were clearly better material for stories, and better remembered over the years. However, Sendings can also be created for beneficial aims, and it is my firm opinion that this is the better option. They can be employed to give protection in a role of active defence, help find lost objects, bring information, or carry out many other tasks. On the other hand, they require some careful thought and consideration if they are not to backfire on you and bring unintended results.

---

[53] Dion Fortune "Psychic Self Defence"

Planning

Before you decide to create a Sending, it is advisable to first run through the planning stage, as with any magical operation. Take your time with this, and write everything down in your Book of Deeds: this will prove an invaluable reference later, and help you to define what it is that you really want. This may already bring out some of the possible traps and pitfalls in your plan. Question whether the situation really requires a magical solution and, if so, whether a Sending is the best type of magical solution. As Sendings can be endowed with a fairly high degree of complexity and intelligence, they are best used for workings of a long-term nature. Assuming that you decide that the situation demands a magical solution, and that a Sending is the best way to proceed, you can go on to formulate the rest.

Firstly, you must accurately define your goal and desire; write it down at length, then try to sum this up in about a dozen words – rambling soliloquies reduce the power of magical intent. Keep your wording positive, eliminating words such as 'no', 'not' and 'never'. For example, it is better to say "I want to be safe" than "I don't want to be attacked." Your subconscious does not understand negatives, and by mentioning the things you wish to avoid you could unwittingly bring them about. Also, try to eliminate all the 'ifs' and 'buts'; if you have to impose too many conditions at this point, it means you have not thought things through properly. Remember that you will be able to instruct your Sending after you have given life to it.

Secondly, concisely write down your desired result and think about all the possible ways in which this could be manifested. These may include some ways that you would not want; if so, note these in writing so that you can limit your Sending later. Formulate your desired result in as few words as possible for effectiveness. Now formulate a distilled *statement of intent*, preferably of no more than four words (eliminating negatives, remember!). This will give you a clue as to the name of your Sending.

Now it is time to define the general and specific realms of influence of your Sending. The general realm of influence is its role in general; the specific realm of influence is its scope of action. I will return to this later when describing a working of my own.

Name and appearance

By now you should have a clear picture of what your Sending is to achieve and how the results are to be manifested. Remember that this is to be a living wight, separate from you but under your control, so it needs to have a name, an appearance, and some kind of physical embodiment (its home, in effect). It will also need feeding in order to maintain its continued existence. You can base the name on your distilled statement of intent, taking the letters, eliminating repetitions and then reorganising them to form a name. Suppose, for example, that the distilled statement of intent (your Sending's core purpose) is "INCREASE SALES", then eliminate the repeating letters as follows: I N C R E A S ~~E~~ ~~S~~ ~~A~~ L ~~E~~ ~~S~~. This leaves you with INCREASL, which can be rearranged to form LIN ACRES, LINACRES, SERCANIL, CRANESIL or some other combination. If you find (as often happens) you are short of vowels to make something pronounceable, feel free to add one or two. An important consideration is that <u>you</u> should feel comfortable with the name. If your gut feeling goes against it, do not use it.

Now for the appearance of your Sending. Let's assume that we decide to use the name LIN ACRES. We could picture her as a high-powered, attractive saleswoman wearing a sharp business suit. Picture everything about her: her face, her hair colour and style, the cut and colour of her suit, her shoes, her height. The main thing is that the appearance should be appropriate to the intended purpose.

Housing and feeding

After deciding on a name and visualising your Sending's form, it is a good idea to have something physical in which to house it. It is not absolutely necessary, but it does provide you with a tangible focus point. Many options are available; you could use a picture, a statuette, a piece of jewellery or a pot. It is often good to have something such as a bottle that can hold a slip of paper or any materials (such as bodily fluids) used in the Sending's creation. You must also decide where this housing is to be kept. It could be on your altar or a shelf of your own home, or it might be secreted close to the target of your intention; only you can decide this, according to your purpose. You will also need a source of psychic energy for your Sending to feed on if it is to remain in existence for long. This can be provided simply by talking to it, and thanking it when it brings a result, but you might wish it to take energy from some other source. I once had a bodyguard entity in the form of a black dog, and I used to give it a dog biscuit daily! Note that it was the act of giving that was important, not the physical biscuits – I used to collect those up every week and give them to the dogs of friends. Going back to our example of Lin Acres the super-saleswoman, it would be appropriate to praise her whenever she got you a sale and to give a 'pep talk' once a week.

Magical abilities and programming

So far, you have defined your Sending's purpose, role and scope of action. You have given it a name, visualised its appearance, decided where its home will be, and decided how you are to feed it. The next step is to define its abilities and embody these in a 'programming symbol'. Our entity Lin Acres, for example, could be given the ability to read people's minds and identify their thoughts and desires, and pick out links between these desires and your service or product. She should also have the power of persuasive speech, and the ability to guide you towards fruitful and cost-effective sales channels (after all, you cannot leave all of it to her!). List these abilities, for you will need to recite them later when you give life to your creation. Finally, it is a good idea to encapsulate her entire purpose and abilities symbolically insofar as possible; this will form the perfect link for your subconscious to interact with. It is at this stage that your knowledge of runes and galdrastafir can come into play. Select the runes that are in harmony with your intention and compose them into a bindrune or magical stave that will embody your intention, the means and the desired result. This symbol will have a power and meaning that is always intelligible to your subconscious, but which your conscious mind will soon forget; its meaning will probably be quite hidden from other minds. Our saleswoman Lin Acres could use the runes *áss* for persuasive speech and the ability to read minds, *ár* for a good return, *sól* for success, and *fé* for the money she will bring you. You might even want to include one of the *kaupaloki* (bargain-sealer) staves. Do not make this symbol over-complicated, as you will need to visualise it and project it into your Sending when birthing it. The symbol may also be carved or painted on the housing, or written on a piece of paper and deposited inside the housing.

Lifespan and termination

How long do you want your Sending to continue in existence? How long does it need to remain in existence? This is something to be built into your instructions at the doom-giving, immediately after the creation. A single-purpose Sending may be set to disperse once its mission is accomplished, but one that has a long-term purpose may need to be given a finite date or occasion – perhaps your own death. In case things do not work out as you wish, or if circumstances change, it is also good to include an immediate termination clause along the lines of "When I say/do this or that, you will cease to exist." Remember also that a long-term Sending may not survive for as long as you wish: magic is not an entirely predictable science. If a Sending appears to have stopped functioning and cannot be revived, it is best to formally terminate it. In all cases, the housing should be ritually destroyed or dismantled when your Sending has accomplished its mission or is formally terminated.

Giving life to your Sending – the working

At last, after all the thought and preparation, everything is nearly ready for the birth of your Sending and for dispatching it to do your will. Just two things remain. You should pick a passage from a mythological (or Biblical if you wish) episode that provides an archetypal alignment with your aim. In all operations involving Sendings, I like to use the passage in the Völuspá in which Odin, Hænir and Lóður give life to two wooden logs and create the first humans from them. In addition, you should write a narrative recitation that brings the future into the past, and describes the working as if it were already achieved. Give full rein to your imagination here, and do not worry if your style of writing is not very good; just do your best. It is also good to prepare a *galdur* (incantation), as described in Chapter 8.

Set up your working area as you normally would, perhaps with the addition of incense that is sympathetic to the aim. Have before you everything you have prepared – the housing for your Sending (e.g. bottle, piece of jewellery or statuette), the words you intend to speak (mythical and narrative recitations, the incantation, and the symbol that embodies your Sending.

1. Calm your mind, excluding all everyday thoughts, then open the proceedings in your usual way. Ritually cleanse[54] anything, such as the housing, that may have undesired past associations.
2. Perform the mythological recitation to align the working with the mythological archetype.
3. Utter the statement of intent, then light the candle.
4. Perform the narrative recitation.

---

54 See Chapter 5.

5. Prepare the housing (the exact way you do this will vary according the purpose and the housing; see the example below to get some idea).
6. Visualise, develop focused intent, and accumulate power. This is perhaps the most crucial stage of the proceedings. Using movement, gesture and incantation, work yourself into a state of magical ecstasy, focusing on your Sending and its purpose to the exclusion of all else. Visualise it taking shape in the centre of your working area until it appears completely real; see it breathe and move. When the moment feels right, 'fire' your prepared symbol into the visualised form to give it life.
7. Address your creature and draw it into its housing; see it voluntarily concentrating and entering the housing. Speak as follows:

> "Wight of my creation, I draw you into this (bottle/jewel/statue etc.); this shall be your home."

You may wish to add a little of your blood to it at this point, and the breath of life.
8. Pronounce the Sending's name and doom.
9. End the rite and clear the working area in your usual way.

Monitoring

As with all your workings, you should periodically monitor the results and make written notes. As ever, be honest. On the other hand, do not dwell too much on your Sending outside of 'feeding time'; let it go about its work and have confidence that its work will be achieved. If it seems to be having undesired results, consider exercising your prepared termination formula.

If all of this seems daunting or overly complex to you, do not be put off. These steps are meant to be a guide, and the results are the main thing. However, I would recommend that you at least give consideration to all of the factors outlined above in order to avoid unintended consequences. My first Sending, sent years ago by force of visualisation and will only, was a black dog to protect my wife and baby son while I was working away all week. It certainly worked: several wasps that crawled into my son's bedroom through an ill-fitting window frame were found, dead and decapitated, on the floor. Unfortunately, my son had nightmares of something dark and frightening, and my wife frequently saw a dark, ominous shape haunting the house. I had not thought things out, so I called back the hound and re-absorbed its energy.

The foregoing example of a Sending named Lin Acres, 'super saleswoman', is fairly anodyne; this was because I wished to emphasise that, unlike those in the old Icelandic folk tales, a Sending need not be bent on death and destruction, and can have a positive purpose. I will tell now, in some detail, of another Sending of my own.

I am lucky enough to have an extensive park and woodland nearby, which I visit every day, rain or shine. An ecologist would describe it as a 'bio-diverse habitat'; to me it is a magical landscape, full of different wights, lines and vortices of power, and mythological associations such as the ash of Woden, the elder of Frau Holle, and the oak of Thunor. It therefore angered me greatly when I noticed an increase of littering and of wanton damage to this place. I could have simply carped about it or written a letter to the local newspaper, but I decided to act in the most effective way open to me. I would create a guardian – a demonic park-keeper – to protect the woods and parkland, wreaking vengeance on miscreants and deterring by terror. Over the period of about a month, I formed a clear image of this guardian and an inner feeling of its essence. I listened again and again to two appropriate pieces of music: the eldritch 'Witch Elder' from the Albion Band's album 'Lark Rise to Candleford', and the ominous, haunting track 'Reaper Man' by Fire + Ice. I spoke to the over-arching spirit of the woods, and to all of its wights, explaining my intention. I asked as many of the tree and shrub wights as possible to participate by donating a leaf to my Sending, gathered the leaves, and found a small bottle to place them in. I like to make a full song of the galdur, so I composed it and rehearsed it, and I chose the name 'Catpore' for the Sending (this was based on its role of protector). Eventually, by the waxing of the Moon and on a Tuesday, I was ready to give life to it. The procedure below is based on my own notes.

Catpore Sending

Raise the Holy Hall. Prepare salted water, and then cleanse the bottle which is to house the entity by Earth, Water, Air, and Fire.

RECITATION:

> *"To the coast then came, kind and mighty,*
> *From the gathered gods three great Aesir.*
> *On the land they found, of little strength,*
> *Ask and Embla, unfated yet.*
> *Sense they possessed not, soul they had not,*
> *Being nor bearing, nor blooming hue.*
> *Soul gave Odin, sense gave Hænir,*
> *Being, Lóður, and blooming hue."*

STATEMENT OF INTENT:

> *"It is my will and intent to give life to a being, a Sending, and send it to protect the park and woods from all harm. I light this candle as a token of my will and intent."*

[Light candle]

NARRATIVE RECITATION:

Read "Catpore the Park-keeper" (This was a fairy-tale type story, in which I narrated the desired effect as if it had already happened.)

PREPARATION OF HOUSING:

Fill bottle with earth, moss, grass, leaves, wood and wine, saying:

> *"I prepare this, the body of my Sending; into it I put the essence of the woods and the parkland: earth, grass, bracken, and the leaves of many trees. To them I add a splinter from a tree that was harmed, for spite and desire for vengeance. To them I add wine, spirit of the wort-world. In this body shall my Sending dwell, thence to fare forth and do his work, until this World ends, unless I recall him."*

ACCUMULATION OF POWER, VISUALISATION AND INTENT:

Walk widdershins around the stead, singing the song, chanting the runes that make up his name, and all the time visualising the Sending in the centre, identifying with him and feeling the hate and desire to destroy the 'orcs' who vandalise and litter the woods and parkland. When sufficient power has been accumulated, fire the bindrune into the visualised Sending.

SPEAK TO SENDING AND GIVE HIM HIS DOOM:

> *"Being of my creation, I draw you into this bottle; this shall be your home. [Prick finger and draw blood] I give life to you; [Breathe FAAA into bottle] I give breath to you; water and earthly body I have given you already. Your form is dreadful – a tall, shambling, black, stick-figure with glowing red eyes. I give you life by fire [pass bottle over candle flame] and remind you of the scent of the woods [pass over pine incense]. And now I pronounce your name and doom.*
>
> *"CATPORE art thou hight, and in this name shalt thou acquire fame. Thou shalt protect the park and the woods – I shall show thee thy bounds upon the morrow – inflicting harm in mind and body to all who wantonly and maliciously desecrate these places. Whenever a branch is broken carelessly, whenever a fire is lit, whenever waste and litter are thrown upon the grass or in the woods, thou shalt awake and*

respond; whenever park furniture is broken or moved without good cause, or flowers trampled, thou shalt awake and respond. These skills I give thee:

- To read minds, based on that which I would discern, to know the difference between malicious intent and otherwise;
- To cause and inflict terrible dread, enough to cause a human to become mad with fear;
- To show thyself in the shadows, in the form I gave thee, the better to inflict fear and dread;
- To cause dead branches to fall on the heads of miscreants;
- To cause brambles to rise up and trap and tear the legs of miscreants;
- To make the grass as a bed of thorns for those who bring litter;
- To learn, and follow my further instructions.

"Thou shalt feed on, and grow stronger from, every ray of sunshine and every drop of rain that falls upon the park and woodland, from every whisper of the wind in the leaves and branches, from the frost and fall of snow in winter, and from the growth of every leaf.

Thou shalt persist forever, warding the park and the woods, unless thy name be said three times backwards, followed by the last verse of the Hávamál in Old Norse.

"On the morrow I will show thee thy bounds, show thee thy dwelling, and send thee to perform thy work. As my will, so mote it be."

CLOSE THE TEMPLE AND WORKING WITH THE USUAL WORDS

The next day, I carried Catpore, within his housing, around the boundaries of his wardship, pointing out and explaining to him what was allowed and not allowed. For example, that he must leave the gardeners alone, and children under the age of twelve. I then hid the bottle, his housing, in the woods. Within a fortnight, the level of littering and vandalism had been reduced by 90%. To my regret, Catpore lived and worked only for about twenty months, but it was not a bad result. When the littering and damage returned, I assessed that Catpore was at the end of his power. I said his name thrice, backwards, recited the Hávamál verse, emptied the bottle and disposed of it.

For more ideas on creating Sendings and other magical entities, read 'Creating Magickal Entities' by David Michael Cunningham (details are in the bibliography).

CHAPTER 14

DIVINATION

Strictly speaking, I do not consider divination an act of magic or sorcery. The latter, in my opinion, is about getting things done and manifesting one's will, while divination is about seeing what has happened (and who may have been involved) and what might happen in the future. However, that is perhaps a nit-picking argument, in the same way that experts will tell you that pterosaurs and plesiosaurs were not really dinosaurs. What is undoubtedly true is that divination can have a role in magical operations. After all, it is always a good idea to take advice on whether your intended working will have the desired effect, and whether it may have some otherwise unforeseen and undesired results. In any serious matter, once you have gone through the process of thinking through the issue that you are addressing (and whether magic is an appropriate solution), it is good to perform an act of divination to discern what the likely result will be if you do nothing of a magical nature. Unless an adverse outcome is indicated, proceed with formulating and refining the intent, and working out the details of the operation. Before actually performing the operation, however, consult the oracle again to find out what is likely to happen as a result; if the outcome looks positive, go ahead, but if it looks negative you may have to re-think matters.

We all have our talents, being stronger in some fields and weaker in others. Compared to some, I have to admit that I am a bit of a dunce when it comes to divination, though I do have my moments, sometimes spontaneously. I have had friends who could not look at a playing card or a piece of broken glass without getting some insight into the future. On the other hand, it was not necessarily a talent to be envied because they were usually somewhat unfocused and so taken up with the constant feed of information that they did not make for good practical magicians. It can often be mutually beneficial for the practically-oriented sorcerer to pair up with a partner who is less focused but more likely to see the broader perspective. Having admitted that divination is not my strong suit, I nevertheless feel that some discussion of the techniques is necessary in a book of this kind. It may surprise you that only two techniques of divination are mentioned in the galdrabækur which I have studied in depth: scrying and oneiromancy.

Scrying

Quite a lot of the entries in the old books of magic are devoted to acts of scrying, often to discover who has stolen something. It seems to be a very old technique, for it is mentioned in the oldest known Icelandic book of magic, AM 434a 12mo 'Lækningakver' dating from around 1500 CE. You can find it in the appendix on traditional Icelandic spells. In essence - and all these spells are very similar - the technique runs as follows. One should take a wooden bowl that has not been previously used, and carve on its bottom (the inside bottom) a certain stave. Then one should fill it with water and, as specified in some versions, sprinkle finely-ground yarrow leaves on the surface of the water. The original operation in 'Lækningakver' requires a few words to be spoken as follows:

> *"I desire, by the nature of the herb and the power of the sign, that I may see the shadow of the one who has stolen from me and others."*

To judge from the number of such entries, one might think that early modern Iceland was in the grip of a theft epidemic. I can only put it down to the fact that policing in the period was minimal to non-existent and that people were therefore thrown back on their own resources when it came to discovering the perpetrator. With this reservation, I think that scrying is a perfectly good and authentic method for those who have a talent for it, and not only for discovering thieves. Peering into a bowl of water is only one way to do it. One can also use a crystal ball or a black mirror; all that is required to produce the latter is to take a picture frame, remove the glass and paint or spray the back of it in black, and then replace it in the frame. I have read that one can obtain the same result from looking at a sheet of black-sprayed sandpaper or looking out into the dark through a glass window with a light behind you. This all leads me to the belief that it is all down to the 'inner eye', and that one could, if suitably gifted, probably simply close one's eyes, tune out, and get the same results.

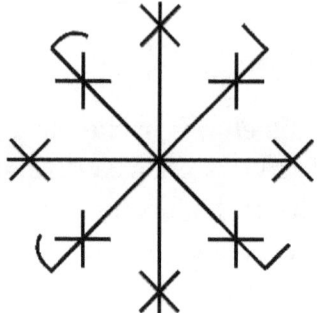

SCRYING STAVE FROM AM 434A 12MO 'LÆKNINGAKVER'

Oneiromancy

This means 'divination by dreaming' and appears to have been a fairly common technique, if one may judge from the number of *draumstafir* or dream-staves which are to be found. Sometimes the intention is to discover a thief (as with the scrying method), but in other cases it is 'to dream what you will'. That could include just about anything, of course, but let us assume that divination is involved. One which I have found to have some effect is the 100th spell in Lbs 2413 8vo, and I will give this in the appendix on traditional spells: "If you want to know what is hidden from the common man.

Carve these staves on brass with steel and lay by your ear and fall asleep and you will experience." I did not find it effective when lying by my ear, so laid it instead on my bedside table, and since then I have often had vivid and unusual dreams, frequently involving galdrastafir.

From Lbs 764 8vo: To dream what you will.

Astragalomancy

Another authentic Icelandic method of divination, though not mentioned in the old books of magic, is to cast the astragalus, or knuckle bone, of a sheep and see which way up it lands. The astragalus is rounded on one side and hollow on the other; the sides are relatively flat. It does not matter to which side you attach a positive or negative connotation, as long as you are consistent. My interpretation is:

Round side up = Yes
Hollow side up = No
On its side = Maybe/Cannot give answer

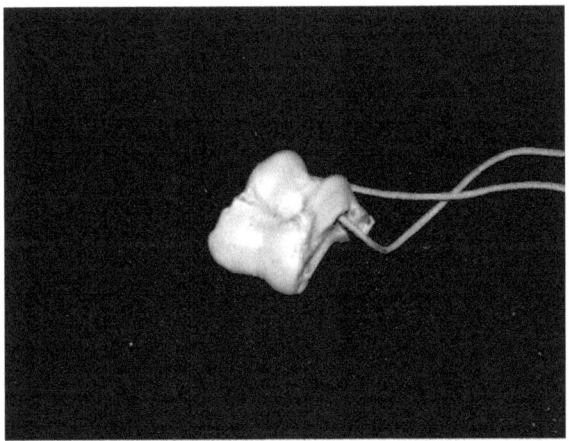

The bone in the photograph was given to me by my friend Benedikt (Bjössi) Petursson when I first visited Iceland in 2008.

Sitting Out (Útisetna)

This is a method of divination well attested in the sagas. It simply involves sitting, or perhaps lying, in isolation in an outside space, and waiting for an answer from the gods to the issue that is troubling you. In the course of sitting out, you can look for omens such as the flight of birds to provide your answer. Regrettably, much lore of omens has been lost today, but you can develop your own on the basis of experience. In the place where I live, we hardly ever see ravens, so crows have to take their place as representatives of Huginn and Muninn. We do have red kites, which I see as taking the place of eagles and giving a sign of victory. Magpies are plentiful, and one can use the lore of the old magpie rhyme ("One for sorrow, two for joy etc.) as a guide, but it must be borne in mind that their numbers are seasonally influenced because they pair in spring for mating, provide flocks of siblings as the chicks leave the nest, and then become solitary in winter. I see pigeons, plump and complacent, as signs of prosperity. If you have some ancient feature such as a standing stone in your vicinity, it is good to use it as your place of sitting out. Some four-and-a-half miles away from my home stands a clump of cup and ring marked rocks, and I have often gone there to sit out. I have always come away with an answer to my question. The journey to them, on foot, gives the operation the aspect of a pilgrimage and helps to calm the mind in advance, and the pleasant feeling of tiredness after the nine-mile round trip gives a feeling of accomplishment and a sense of having made an offering of effort. Be sure to take warm clothes and something soft and insulating to sit on in inclement weather!

Using the Runes

This is not really an authentically early modern method of divination, but it is one that better suits my limited psychic abilities. As I am not even trying, in this case, to stick to methods prevailing in the 16th or 17th Centuries, I use the 24 runes of the Elder Futhark as these give a wider selection than the rather restrictive 16 runes of the Younger Futhark. I have two sets: the pasteboard cards which I mentioned in Chapter 4, and set of 24 wooden lots which I carved and stained many years ago. There are various ways to consult the wisdom of the runes. For a quick answer to a simple question, you can select a single card or lot at random and then meditate on its message according to the lore given in the rune poems (see Chapter 3). A three-rune spread can give a little more detail, of course. My favourite method, which I routinely use before performing any consequential magical operation, is to select nine wooden lots at random and then cast them onto a marked cloth. Before casting, I recite the 111th verse of the Hávamál (Lay of the High One) to bring the exercise into a mythic context:

> *"It is time to sing on the sage's seat*
> *at Urth's well.*
> *I saw and was silent, I watched and thought.*
> *I heard the speech of men, I heard talk of runes.*
> *They were not silent at council.*
> *At Hár's hall, in Hár's hall*
> *I heard them speak."*

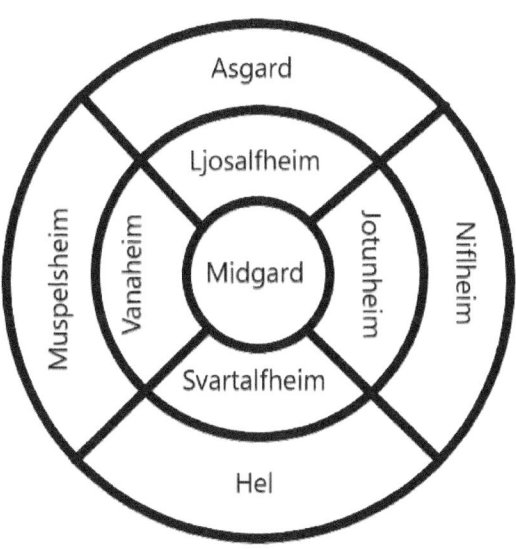

With the 24 lots face-down before me, I look upward and select nine of them by feel alone. Then I roll and shake them in my cupped hands, and with the words "Runes, rown right rede!" I cast them onto the cloth. Any lots which fall outside the outermost circle are ignored, though it is still worth looking at them as factors which might have presented themselves but be can be safely ignored. The rest are read according to their places on the cloth and in relation to each other. The cloth should - at least in the mind's eye - appear like this:

It is, of course, a representation of the nine worlds of Yggdrasil, and I assign the following meanings to the nine zones:

Zone	Meaning
Midgard	Immediate, everyday concerns, the here and now. Runes which fall into this central circle should be read first, and they indicate the most pressing matters.
Liosalfheim	The arts and the intellect; matters of the mind; the rede of the Light Elves.
Svartalfheim	Industry; money matters; manual creativity; but also the emotions; the rede of the Dark Elves (Dwarfs).
Asgard	Spirituality; matters of religion; the higher self; the rede of the Aesir.
Hel	The sleepy realm of the dead; matters that are dormant, "on the back burner"; the rede of the Ancestors.
Vanaheim	Organic growth; fertility; farming; the rede of the Vanir.
Jotunheim	Sudden changes; turmoil; destruction; setbacks; the rede of the Etins.
Muspelsheim	Fiery, expansive energy; rapid expansion; warning to be careful about moving too fast.
Niflheim	Icy contraction; plans on hold; obstruction.

The message from each rune should be read according to its intrinsic meaning, its place on the cloth, and its position in relation to other runes. For example, Fehu in Niflheim may indicate that you will not be getting a pay rise any time soon; if also close to Dagaz, it may indicate that you will soon get revelations of how to escape that situation. Be sure to make careful notes (including your interpretation) and a sketch of the cast so that you can refer to it later. Sometimes it is better to get someone else who is suitably skilled to read the runes for you, it being generally acknowledged that it is harder to read them for yourself than for others because you are usually too close to the situation. When you have finished your reading, put away the lots with care and reverence; they are, after all, your treasured advisors.

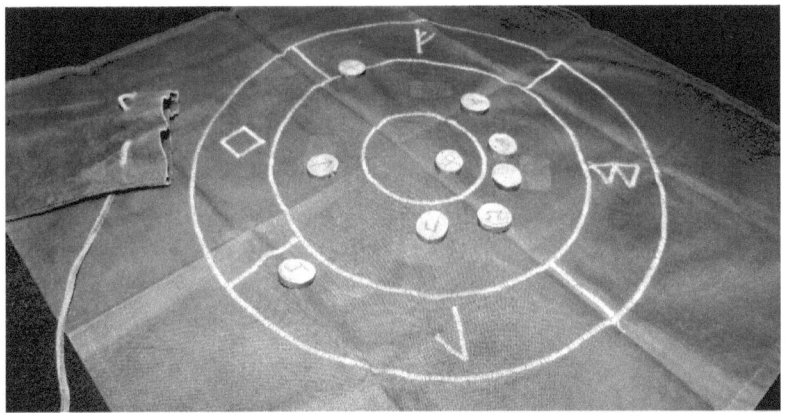

My own lots and casting-cloth.
The runes embroidered on the cloth are of no significance.

Unless, for some physical reason, you are unable to do so, always make sure to create your own rune-lots for casting. They will have much more power than anything you can buy. The best woods to use are rowan, ash and yew. Be careful with yew, because every part of the tree is poisonous; never leave yew lots where pets or small children might get at them.

For more information on divination using the runes, read "At the Well of Wyrd" by Edred Thorsson (see bibliography).

CHAPTER 15

WASHING RITUALS AND THE HELM OF AWE

Many readers will already be familiar with the Ægishjálmur, or Helm of Awe. The most famous of the Icelandic magical staves, it is widely used today as a tattoo, for marketing, and even as the logo of an entire Icelandic district (Strandir). It is most often depicted in the form that is to be found in Lbs 143 8vo 'Galdrakver' from around 1670, and many people assume that this is its one and only form. Personally, I feel that the symbol is today vastly over-used, misunderstood and commercially over-exploited in a way which does not do justice to the power and subtlety of its operation.

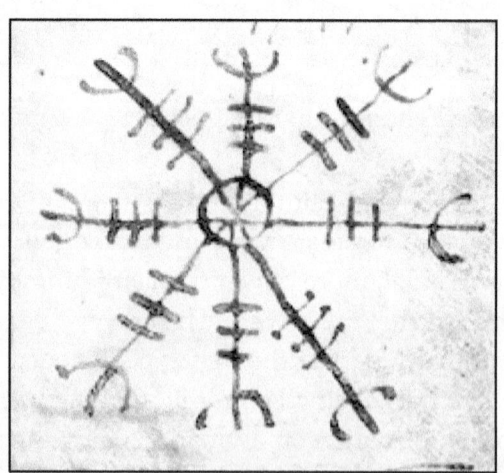

HELM OF AWE FROM LBS 143 8VO 'GALDRAKVER'

A diligent reading of but a few of the old books of magic will reveal that the Helm of Awe symbol can take many forms, as shown in the illustrations below:

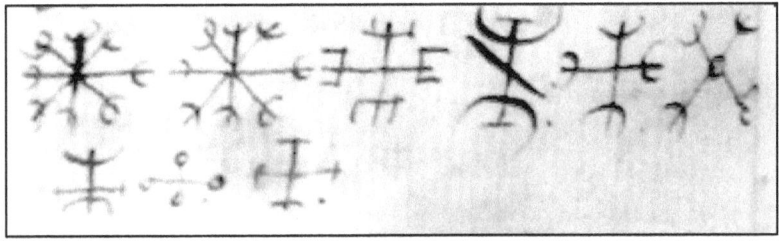

9 Helms of Awe from Lbs 2413 8vo

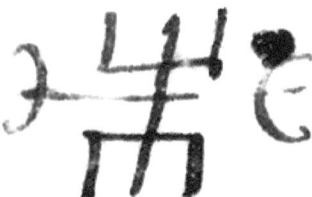

A Helm of Awe from the Stockholm MS

A Helm of Awe in AM 434a 12mo 'Lækningakver'

As with many staves that are to be found in the old books of magic, the same stave-forms were sometimes also used for different purposes but, as a Helm of Awe working, the intention is generally consistent wherever it is found:

- To avert the scorn and anger of powerful men;
- To have one's debts discharged;
- To gain the love and respect of others.

In 2015, I wrote:

"The majority of the intentions given above reveal a number of prime factors when it comes to the helm of awe. Firstly, it is the working of a friendless underling, a 'Billy no-mates' if you like, who is oppressed by powerful men and possibly pursued for bad debts. Secondly, it is often associated with ritual washing to wash away the anger and enmity of these powerful men. Thirdly, the sorcerer aims to gain general popularity. Finally, in such workings, the stave should always be traced or projected (by visualisation) on the forehead "between the brows". One should by no means think ill of anyone who uses the working to escape this unenviable position; after all, magic is frequently (though not exclusively) the resort of those lacking the physical or financial means to achieve their aims. On the other hand, it does not tie in well with any modern use of the symbol (e.g. as a tattoo) in an attempt to project a 'tough guy' image, and bearing it on any part of the body other than the forehead is, frankly, meaningless.[55]"

It might be concluded that this working holds little value for someone who has no debts, is not particularly unpopular, and has nothing to fear from a powerful overlord. However, if we go further to consider the *technique* of the operation rather than its specific intent, we can gain a valuable magical tool. Firstly, note that this is primarily a washing ritual, as we can see from the first lines of the spell in 'Lækningakver':

---

[55] Christopher Alan Smith 'Icelandic Magic', pages 165-166.

> *"Wash yourself in water three times and read the Lord's Prayer in between, and say this three times:*
> *'I wash from me my enemies' hatred,*
> *the greed and wrath of powerful men,*
> *that they may happily come to meet me*
> *and look me in the eyes laughing."*

Now, with all due respect to the people of early modern Iceland, they were not a particularly clean lot unless they had the fortune to have a hot spring close to their dwelling[56]. A bit of a splash with cold water using cupped hands was often the closest they got to a good wash for most of the year. These days, most of us have the luxury of a shower and/or a bath, and we can make a ritual of our daily shower. Secondly, why should we have to limit ourselves to a specific intention which is not necessarily appropriate to our circumstances? To ignore the potential of a useful technique would be a waste, and the best of magicians are adaptive and inventive. The solution is to bring the entire Helm of Awe working up to date. Just consider that, whenever you take a shower or bath, you are working with two of the classic, magical elements, water and fire, and is that not quite wonderful in itself? You can adapt all or any of the words of this rite to suit your own circumstances, but this is the form of ritual which I use every morning.

(Turning on the shower and waiting for the water to run hot, I say:)

> *"May this water, and the fire that heats it, be blessed*
> *in the names of Odin, Vili and Vé!"*

(then, after washing, I stand under the running water and say:),

> *"In the names of Odin, Vili and Vé,*
> *and by the power of the holy Fire and Water,*
> *I shower myself with health;*
> *I shower myself with wealth;*

---

56 Read Chapter 2 of Alda Sigmundsdóttir's 'The Little Book of the Icelanders in the Old Days' for more details.

> *I shower myself with love and happiness;*
> *I shower myself with luck.*

(Making the sign of the Helm of Awe on my forehead)

> *"On my brow I bear the Helm of Awe;*
> *all men love and respect me,*
> *and are eager to do my bidding.*
> *All these things are and shall be mine*
> *for all the length of my days,*
> *and the length of my days will be long.*
> *So shall it be!"*

The working is all the more effective when it employs a good deal of visualisation, so, for example, when you say "I shower myself with health", picture yourself feeling very well, strong and fit, and free of anything which may ail you. When tracing the Helm of Awe on your forehead, it is a good idea to use one of its simpler forms such as the four-armed one with trident terminations.

In summary, I consider the Helm of Awe working to represent a valuable magical technique that can be quite versatile in its applications. You can also use ritualised washing in the same way for other intentions, whether to rid yourself of something or to shower yourself with blessings.

CHAPTER 16

A SAMPLE WORKING

Much information has been given so far concerning all the elements which come into consideration when planning and performing a magical operation. However, this information has of necessity been delivered in a rather fragmented form. My intention in this chapter, therefore, is to present you with a notional working, from its initial conception to the ultimate review of its effects.

Stage 1: Planning and Preparation

Obviously, the performance of a magical working has to fulfil some need, otherwise there would not be much point in doing it. You might, for example, feel that you need more money, or a home of your own, or a girlfriend or boyfriend. The first question to ask yourself is "Am I really addressing the right issue?" Sometimes deeper thought can expose the issue which really needs addressing. Why do you need more money? Is it because you cannot cover your monthly bills, or is it because you simply want to acquire more material possessions when you already have a house full of them? Or perhaps you want money to satisfy an insatiable partner and family, while you would actually be satisfied with a less extravagant lifestyle. All these things require thought, for if you aim magic at the wrong issue it will not bring you happiness. The second question to ask is "Do I really need to use magic to achieve my aim?" It may be that the answer to your predicament is blindingly simple. For example, the lack of a girlfriend or boyfriend may be down to the fact that you are desperately shy, and never make an effort to meet or mingle with others; in which case, it is confidence that you need (though magic can help with that).

Let us assume that you have properly considered the perceived need, and have done everything that can reasonably be expected of you to fulfil it by 'normal' measures. You therefore turn to magic to move things along. For this sample working, let us pretend you are a would-be writer who cannot bring up the inspiration required to pen the project in hand, be it a book or a school essay. Being a well-trained magician, you open your Book of Deeds and enter the date, the intention ("To Gain Inspiration") and a quick summary of the background. Then you list the considerations, one by one. In this case, you can dispense with the 'before' and 'after' divinations, as the operation only affects yourself and some inspiration can only be beneficial.

- What kind of magic is required here[57]? Let us assume this is a recurring problem that calls for a long-term solution. The target is yourself, so it would be good to have a talisman that you can wear all the time, or at least whenever you are writing. You decide to create a paper talisman that you can keep in your wallet or hang around your neck in a container on a cord.
- To which deity (if any) should I appeal for help? Here Odin is clearly indicated, being the master of writing, poetry and inspiration. You therefore decide to include an appeal to Odin as part of your working. The old boy loves a drop of mead, so - note to self - buy mead on next shopping trip. (If you really would prefer a Christian theme, which is entirely in accordance with 17th-century Icelandic magic - you can also appeal to the Archangel Raphael and to St Francis de Sales, the patron saint of writers. If you wish, you can even evoke all three - Odin, Raphael and St Francis de Sales - for a truly authentic working in the spirit of early modern eclecticism!)

---

[57] See Chapter 11, The Methods of Delivery.

- What is your galdor, your incantation, to be? You have read the Poetic Edda, and decide that verse 141 of the Hávamál is really appropriate for aligning your rite with mythic narrative:

    "Then I began to grow
    and waxed well in wisdom.
    One word led me to another,
    one work led me to another."

- That's fine for the first part, but how is the rest of your galdor to read? You have not performed your working yet, so you are not yet feeling inspired. However, you know from the Eddas that the holy mead of inspiration was made from the blood of Kvasir, that it was won by Odin, and that its name is Óðrerir[58] (stirrer of divine madness or inspiration). So you write your incantation as follows:

    "Blood of Kvasir came to me,
    Stirrer of inspiration;
    Filled me and infused me
    With divine exhilaration!"

- We can add some rune-galdor to this once we have decided which runes to use.
- In what bindrune or galdrastaf are you going to embody your intention? You could look at creating a bindrune from the runes of the Elder Futhark, and there would be nothing wrong with that but, as this is mainly a book on Icelandic magic, let us raise the difficulty ratio a little and go for a galdrastaf. That restricts us to the Younger Futhark or the later, extended Futhark for our runes. The first which recommends itself is *Áss* (ᚨ), being in effect a name of Odin, the god of inspiration. The second is *Nauð* (ᚾ), for the kindling of the flame from friction. The third is a little more difficult. It is so tempting to use the Elder Futhark *Kenaz* for the concept of a steady, controlled

---

[58] Pronounced 'oathe-re-reer'.

flame, but that does not accord with our early modern theme and the meaning of *Kaun* in the Old Icelandic Rune Poem. So let us instead go for the fair, guiding light of the sun in *Sól* (ᛋ). This leads us to the formula ANS, and allows you to flesh out your invocation with the rune-galdor "Aaaannnnsssss". Furthermore, it gives you three runes on which to base your galdrastaf. You decide that you want to bind the runes together on one shaft, with ᚼ and ᛁ grouped along the shaft, and ᛋ crossing it at the end. The result looks like this:

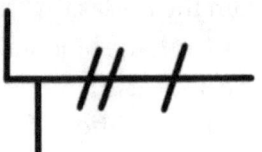

Then you decide you want to invoke this divine inspiration from all eight outer worlds, so a radial stave will be best. Placing a circle at the centre to represent yourself, you add the above sigil in all eight directions. Finally, you 'flatten out' the bars of the *Áss* (ᚼ) and *Nauð* (ᛁ) runes so that they cross the radial shafts at 90 degrees, simply to improve the aesthetic appearance. The final galdrastafur appears like this:

- Now all that remains to be decided is when, and where, to create your talisman. You decide to create it in your own stead and on a Wednesday, this being Woden's (Odin's) day, while the moon is waxing.

Stage 2: The Working

On the appointed day, you go to your stead and prepare to execute the working. Your stead should be as clean and tidy as you can make it, and the harrow (altar) should be set up in the north with your dedicated cloth covering the mundane platform (e.g. coffee table) to transform it into a sacred space. On the harrow you should have everything you require: candles on tall holders to signal the start of the ritual, and to provide illumination; matches; a source of incense; a pen or felt-tip (preferably with red ink); and the slip of paper with your galdrastaf already lightly traced on it in pencil. There should also be a vessel (horn, glass or cup) containing a quantity of mead - enough for two mouthfuls - and a libation dish. You should have washed or showered recently and put on clean clothes. For best effects, you should not have eaten too recently, as a full stomach can make you feel heavy and sleepy; on the other hand, do not make yourself so hungry as to be distracted.

You enter your stead and put all else out of your mind. You perform the opening rite, as described in Chapter 6, pause for a moment and, with arms upraised, address Odin.

> *"Allfather, Odin, Master of Inspiration!*
> *I call upon you to help me in this rite!"*

Raising the vessel of mead, you say "To Odin!" and take a mouthful of mead, swallowing it with three gulps[59]. What remains of the mead, you pour into the libation dish. Next you commence your incantation:

---

[59] Representing Odin's swallowing of the mead from the 3 vessels, Odrerir, Son and Bodn.

> *"Then I began to grow*
> *and waxed well in wisdom.*
> *One word led me to another,*
> *one work led me to another.*
> *Blood of Kvasir came to me,*
> *Stirrer of inspiration;*
> *Filled me and infused me*
> *With divine exhilaration!*
> *Aaaannnnssss*
> *Aaaannnnssss*
> *Aaaannnnssss*[60]*."*

As you chant the rune-galdur "Aaaannnnssss", *see* and *feel* the power of the runes flowing into you from outside, and amassing in your midriff. Continuing to chant, you now draw in ink over the prepared pencil lines of your talisman, feeling the power of the respective runes flowing from your centre, along your arm and into the ink as it flows onto the paper. When the stave has been drawn, you trace in the same way with your finger (without quite touching the image), projecting the individual runes in their respective places on each radial branch. Finally, you see the completed stave shining with a bright light, and you visualise the power flowing inwards to you, the central circle.

Now you take the talisman gently in your cupped hands and visualise a blue field of force surrounding it, similar to the sphere which surrounds your stead. It is permeable, containing the talisman's energy but allowing it to flow out gradually to you. You give it a name, such as 'Inspiration-stirrer', and declare:

> *"Wight of my making,*
> *Ever shall you move my wōd*
> *And give the inspiration I need."*

Above all, have confidence. *Know*, at that moment, that the result is assured, a given fact. The talisman being complete, you finish by thanking Odin and performing the

---

[60] The 'a' sound in 'Aaaannnnssss' is actually pronounced like the 'o' in 'horse'.

closing rite. In this case, you should draw all the generated power into yourself. You snuff the candles, make sure that the incense can burn out safely, tidy away all your magic paraphernalia, and write up your notes while taking a drink and a bite to eat. The mead that was poured as a libation should preferably be poured onto a favourite spot in your garden. If you do not have a garden, then pour it onto a window box or potted plant. If you don't have any of these, just drink and don't make a libation - it's a shame to waste it!

Stage 3: Monitoring

In this phase, which may last for several months, it is important not to dwell on your working at first. Put it out of your mind and try to forget, if possible, that you did it. Keep your talisman safe and close to you at all times, but do not constantly examine it. After about a month, however, you can review the result and write about it in your diary. Has your creative output increased in quantity and quality? It is vitally important to be honest in this matter, otherwise you devalue your efforts. Magic can be capricious, and part of its charm and attraction is that it does not always work. Stick at it, though, and you will begin to notice that you obtain the desired result more frequently than would be indicated by mere chance.

CHAPTER 17

'INSTANT' MAGIC

In the previous chapter, I described how one might make a talisman by an operation of ritual magic. The assumption was that you have the time, leisure, tools, and a convenient space to perform such a ritual. But what about all the occasions when the need arises right now, and you are far from home? You cannot stop and say "Hang on everyone, I need to set up my stead, light some candles, and perform a ritual." No, you need to do something at that given moment, and with whatever tools come to hand - which, in the main, will come down to your own mind, memory and body. Such occasions will greatly outnumber those in which you have time to prepare. It is for this reason that, as already stated, I am a minimalist when it comes to magic, and a great believer that the effective magician is one who can act flexibly, positively and inventively in any situation.

Sometimes, of course, you may have some advance warning, perhaps a few hours or a day, that a requirement for magic will arise; that is why, in Chapter 5, I emphasised the usefulness of a small, portable tool-kit contained in a satchel. In such cases, you may be able to perform a short ritual in your hotel room[61] or some other place where you can get a modicum of privacy. If you do not have even this minimal tool-kit with you, but you have a quiet place (such as the multi-faith prayer room at an airport), you can perform an entire ritual by visualisation alone, using imagination: seeing the candles, smelling the incense, performing the actions, and

---

61 Tip: Do not use incense in hotel rooms. It can trigger fire alarms and attract unwanted attention from the hotel staff.

saying the words silently in your head while you appear to outsiders to be merely sitting in quiet prayer and contemplation. Such a level of visualisation calls for a very strong imagination, and usually the memory and experience of previously having physically performed such rituals.

On other occasions you may have little or no time to prepare, and this is where the 'finger and spittle' method of the old Icelandic spells comes in handy. One of these, to win in gaming (primarily in card games), is shown in Appendix 5. All that is necessary for these is that you should know the form of the stave in advance, and be able to discreetly apply it to yourself or to your target. This method was also traditionally used in order to change the disposition of others: for example, to gain friendship or to assuage the wrath of an enemy. Visualisation is also needed here, for you must 'see' the stave that you trace, even though it is virtually invisible to anyone else. The method can also be used to create and project new bindrunes and staves of your own making, and I already mentioned an instance of this in Chapter 11 under 'Direct Carving'. Think of the rune, or runes, which will accomplish your aim, draw them into you by breathing to infuse them into your being, trace them in spittle on your palm, and then blow across your palm to send them on their way.

I have already stressed the need to have utter confidence that your spell will work; some of the old Icelandic spells call on the sorcerer to "have great faith", by which they meant confidence and imagination rather than religious faith. This is where my final method comes in, one which does not employ any runes or galdrastafir but does require a high level of training, experience, and power. With this method, you simply see your desired intention as realised, beyond the shadow of a doubt. It helps to encapsulate your intention in a few terse words - no more than three - devoid of conditions and free of negatives. Because it requires a mindset that can usually be achieved only after years of dedicated practice in other forms of sorcery, it is best to focus at first on small, achievable objectives such as crossing the road without impedance or finding a seat on a crowded train. I consider this the *summa cum laude* of the magician's art, for it is evidence of the ability to make objective reality conform to the will - simply by willing it. It should go without saying that such power can be dangerous, and that one must first achieve complete control over one's emotions. As the saying goes, be careful what you wish for.

With that last admonition hopefully ringing in your ears, you have now come to the end of this book. I can teach you no more; the rest is up to you. Practise diligently, and read widely from the books cited in the bibliography. The quest for Rúna - the Great Mystery - is unending, a sometimes-arduous journey towards an ever-receding horizon, but it is a challenging and exhilarating journey that is well worth embarking on.

APPENDICES

APPENDIX 1

THE RUNE GILD

Founded by Edred Thorsson (Stephen Edred Flowers) in 1980, the Rune Gild is an initiatory school devoted to the esoteric and exoteric study of the runes, the holy mysteries at the heart of ancient Germanic culture. The Rune-Gild strives to nurture its members in their intellectual and spiritual pursuits. It acts as a catalyst for the mastery of knowledge, acquisition of wisdom, and overcoming of obstacles—all in accord with the mythic paradigm established by Oðin, the first and foremost runemaster. If you are drawn toward the goals and work of the Gild, its official online gateway for information and contact can be found at www.rune-gild.org. The Gild offers a full and comprehensive training curriculum via The Nine Doors of Midgard, supplemented by the Gildisbók (the latter is available only to members). Members initially register as Associates, and this gives access to select portals of the online Rune Gild Forum. Upon satisfactory completion of the first two Doors (chapters) of The Nine Doors of Midgard, Associates are eligible to apply to an established Master to be taken on as a Learner. If accepted, the Learner receives tuition, encouragement and guidance from that Master, and also has access to the international moots which are held from time to time. He or she is expected to submit quarterly progress reports, covering specific aspects of training. From there one may expect to progress to the status of Fellow and eventually to Rune-Master. Do note that this is not an undertaking to be given lightly; there is little point in applying to become a Learner unless you are committed to applying yourself to the curriculum and eventually becoming a Master yourself - a process that can take many years.

APPENDIX 2

THE RUNE ROWS

These are the main Futhark rows. Do note that there was never, in any one period, a 'standard' row. Some runes were carved differently in certain inscriptions, they were sometimes mirrored, and the entire rows might be written from right to left, all of which can make life rather difficult for the exoteric runologist. Runes were also written in various coded forms, such a series of vertical scratches, short and long, representing, for example, "the third rune in the first aett". For a more detailed discussion of the various possibilities, readers are referred to R.I. Page's book 'Runes' (see bibliography).

1. The Elder Futhark

This is the oldest known rune-row, and represents the Futhark as it was used from about 250 CE to 700 CE. There are 24 characters, traditionally divided into 3 'aettir', or groups. The sequence is generally consistent in the old inscriptions, but some reverse the positions of the final two runes, Dagaz and Othala. The rune names are reconstructed proto-Germanic names on the basis of etymological research. This row is the one most universally used and referred to by modern, esoteric runers.

Aett	Character	Name	Meaning	Phonetic value
First aett	ᚠ	Fehu	Livestock, wealth	F
	ᚢ	Uruz	Aurochs	U
	ᚦ	Thurisaz	Thurs, giant	TH
	ᚨ	Ansuz	Ancestral god	A
	ᚱ	Raiðo	Riding	R
	ᚲ	Kenaz	Torch	K
	ᚷ	Gebo	Gift, giving	hard G
	ᚹ	Wunjo	Joy	W
Second aett	ᚺ	Hagalaz	Hail	H
	ᚾ	Nauðiz	Need	N
	ᛁ	Isa	Ice	I (pr. 'ee')
	ᰦ	Jera	Year	Y, as in 'year'
	ᛇ	Eihwaz	Yew	EI, as in '<u>gei</u>st'
	ᛈ	Perthro	Lot-cup	P
	ᛉ	Elhaz	Elk	Z
	ᛋ	Sowilo	Sun	S
Third aett	ᛏ	Tiwaz	Týr (the god)	T
	ᛒ	Berkano	Birch	B
	ᛖ	Ehwaz	Horse	E
	ᛗ	Mannaz	Man, mankind	M
	ᛚ	Laguz	Sea, lake	L
	ᛜ	Ingwaz	Ing (the god)	NG, as in 'thi<u>ng</u>'
	ᛞ	Dagaz	Day	D
	ᛟ	Othala	Estate, heritage	O

2. The Anglo-Frisian Futhorc

After the Migration Period, the Elder Futhark underwent a peculiar expansion among the Anglo-Saxons and their cousins across the North Sea in Frisia, and the Old English Rune Poem has more elements in it to reflect this expansion. This may have been for linguistic reasons - the rune phonemes being added to reflect greater subtlety in the pronunciation of the language - but the esoteric glosses for the added runestaves are worth studying. Note that the designation 'Futhorc', with a 'c' instead of a 'k', is merely a convention because it was written so in the Cottonian manuscript for the rune 'Cen'. It was still pronounced as 'k'. The use of runes persisted for a surprisingly long time in the British Isles, even until the 11th Century.

Aett	Character	Name	Meaning	Phonetic value
First aett	ᚠ	Feoh	Wealth	F
	ᚢ	Ur	Aurochs	U
	ᚦ	Thorn	Thorn	TH/Ð
	ᚩ	Os	God	O
	ᚱ	Rad	Riding	R
	ᚳ	Cen	Torch	K or CH
	ᚷ	Gyfu	Gift	hard G
	ᚹ	Wynn	Joy	W
Second aett	ᚺ	Haegl	Hail	H
	ᚾ	Nyd	Need	N
	ᛁ	Is	Ice	I (pr. 'ee')
	ᛄ	Ger (pr. 'Yer')	Harvest	Y, as in 'year'
	ᛇ	Eoh	Yew	?
	ᛈ	Peorth	Lot-cup	P
	ᛉ	Eolhx	Elk's sedge	X (?)
	ᛋ	Sigel	Sun	S
Third aett	ᛏ	Tir	Tir	T
	ᛒ	Beorc	Birch	B
	ᛖ	Eh	Horse	E
	ᛗ	Man	Man, mankind	M
	ᛚ	Lagu	Water	L
	ᛝ	Ing	Ing (the god)	NG, as in 'thi<u>ng</u>'
	ᛞ	Daeg	Day	D

		Ethel	Estate	OE, as in German "schoen"
Supernumary	ᚪ	Ac	Oak	A
	ᚫ	Aesc	Ash	AE, as in German "Maedchen"
	ᚣ	Yr	Bow	Y
	ᛡ	Ior	Snake	IO
	ᛠ	Ear	Grave	EA.

This is only the 29-stave row! It was even extended to 33 staves at one stage.

3. The Younger Futhark

While the English and Frisians were busy extending their rune row, the Scandinavians were doing exactly the opposite. For reasons that are unclear, the Scandinavian rune row contracted from 24 to 16 characters. This meant that some characters had to represent more than one sound, as will be seen from the table below. This is the row which was in use at the time when Norsemen settled Iceland in the late 9th Century. The system of 'aettir' was maintained, but the first aett contracted to 6 characters, while the second and third aettir each contracted to five. The 'doubling up' of phonemes makes it hard to interpret the numerous inscriptions of the period (as on Swedish memorial stones), and one must be something of an expert in Old Norse to make sense of them. Note that, for the sake of brevity, only the names and meanings given in the Old Icelandic Rune Poem are quoted here.

Aett	Character	Name	Meaning	Phonetic value
First aett	ᚠ	Fé	Gold	F
	ᚢ	Úr	Drizzle	U/O
	ᚦ	Þurs	Thurs (giant)	TH/Ð
	ᚬ	Óss	A god	O (a nasal phoneme)
	R	Reið	Riding	R
	ᚴ	Kaun	Sore	K/G
Second aett	ᚼ	Haegl	Hail	H
	ᚾ	Nauð	Need	N
	I	Ís	Ice	I (pr. 'ee')
	ᛆ	Ár	Harvest	A, Á, Æ
	ᛋ	Sól	Sun	S
Third aett	ᛏ	Týr	Týr	T/D
	B	Bjarkan	Birch	B/P
	ᛘ	Maðr	Man, mankind	M
	ᛚ	Lögr	Water	L
	ᛦ	Ýr	Yew	final -R

4. The later, extended Icelandic Futhark

After the conversion of Iceland to Christianity in 1000 CE, Christian priests brought literacy to the country with the use of the Roman alphabet. In the mediaeval and early modern periods, some sought to bring the Futhark on a par with the Roman alphabet by extending the row. This was done using dots or bars, added to the existing characters of the Younger Futhark. This system appears to have been used by magicians and, later, by antiquarians. The traditional Futhark sequence seems to have been lost, and with it the system of aettir. I have only seen it cited in the sequence of the alphabet that is used in Iceland.

ᚨ	ᛒ	ᛏ	ᛂ	ᚠ	ᚠ	ᛣ	ᛁ	ᚴ	ᛚ	ᛦ	ᚼ	ᚾ	ᛒ	ᚱ	ᛋ	ᛏ	ᚢ	ᚦ	ᚧ
a/	b	d	e	f	g	h	i/	k	l	m	n	o	p	r	s	t	u	þ	ö
á/							j/										/	/	
æ							y										v	ð	

In some texts, the letter v is represented by ᚠ rather than ᚢ.

APPENDIX 3

OF MÁLRÚNIR AND THE RUNE-KENNINGS

In realising what a can of worms I was about to open, I was tempted to omit this appendix altogether. However, I did promise some readers of my book "Icelandic Magic" that I would give the subject some consideration in my next book (i.e. this one), and I feel duty-bound to fulfil that promise. The issue of málrúnir and rune-kennings arises for those who have already gone a little deeper into Icelandic magic, and have perhaps read some of the original manuscripts or, at least, Dr Stephen Flowers' book "Icelandic Magic" (2016) or Skuggi's (Jochum Eggertsson's) "Galdraskræða" from 1940 (now available in translation as "The Sorcerer's Screed" - see bibliography). The málrúnir are quoted in several of the old texts, sometimes simply as lists of alternative magical (or perhaps merely cryptic) characters, but at other times accompanied by 'kennings'. These are highly intriguing, but we have to ask ourselves some pertinent questions:
- What are we to understand by '*málrúnir*'?
- What can the kennings tell us, if anything?
- What relationship exists between the kennings and the various unorthodox rune-rows that accompany them?
- Do they have any practical use for magicians in the Northern Tradition?

The Sources

Málrúnir are accompanied by context in very few of the sources. To date, I have been able to identify only three of these. The earliest reference is to be found in the Prose Edda of Snorri Sturluson:

> "Þetta er dróttkvæðr háttr. Með þeima hætti er flest ort þat er vandat er. Þessi er upphaf allra hátta, sem *málrúnar eru fyrir oðrum rúnar.*"
> "This is dróttkvaett form. This is the form most often used for elaborate poetry. This is the foundation of all verse-forms just as *speech-runes are the principal sort of runes.*[62]"

Alas, Snorri does not expand on this oblique reference; his main concern was to write a book of instruction for poets so that traditional forms of Icelandic poetry should not die out, not to create a manual of runology. The assertion that *málrúnir* are the principal sort of runes is interesting, but does not tell us what they are, or why they come before other runes.

The next reference is in the Sigrdrífumál, part of the Poetic Edda. It is to be found in the Codex Regius, which probably dates from the early 14th Century. In verse 12 (or 11, or 13, depending on which version you read), Sigrdrífa says to Sigurð:

> "Málrúnar skaltu kunna
> ef þú vilt, at manngi þér
> heiftum gjaldi harm:
> þær of vindr,
> þær of vefr,
> þær of setr allar saman,
> á því þingi,
> er þjóðir skulu
> í fulla dóma fara."
> "Speech-runes learn | that none may seek
> To answer harm with hate;
> Well he winds | and weaves them all,
> And sets them side by side,
> At the judgement-place, | when justice there

---

62 Translation by Anthony Faulkes. The italics are mine, for emphasis.

The folk shall fairly win.[63]"

This potentially tells us a lot more about the purpose of *málrúnir*, and I shall return to it later.

The third (and, so far, the last) instance is the ending of a magical spell contained in Manuscript Lbs 2413 8vo in the archive of the Icelandic National and University Library. The instructions tell how to make a special ink in order to write an adjuration that will ensure a girl marries no-one, but will burn with love for the spell-caster. It ends "…og skrifa í málrúnum" – and write in *málrúnir*. Other sources for the *málrúnir*, though more numerous, are regrettably devoid of context.

So, what actually are *málrúnir*? The term is universally translated as "speech-runes", but few have questioned the meaning of the term, let alone come up with a meaningful explanation of it. A bland reply would be that they are runes which are spoken, but this alone is unfulfilling. All the Futhark runes have a phonetic element to them, and are therefore connected to speech as well as writing. The translation is definitely accurate at a certain level, for the word *mál* (n.) undoubtedly translates into English as 'speech' or 'language' (*tungumál*), but that is not the only possible translation of the word. It can also mean 'matter', 'issue', or 'case', as in a legal case or lawsuit. The derivation is undoubtedly from the image of someone speaking, on their own behalf or another's, when presenting a lawsuit or a defence in a court of law. My contention, based on the Sigrdrífumál quotation above, is that the term *málrúnir* was originally used to refer to spells - runes in the sense of 'mysteries' - that could be used to endow a person with fair and persuasive speech, a 'silver tongue' if you like, when presenting one's case at the Thing, the place of judgement. Only later, after much of the magical lore had been lost, was it taken by antiquarian collectors to refer to cryptic and unorthodox runic characters. It should be remembered that, even in the 17th Century, the old, fading lore was being

---

63 Bellows' translation.

collected and written into manuscripts by people who were not necessarily magicians but wished to record curiosities before they were lost entirely. As Alessa Bauer wrote in 2010[64]:

> *"Grundsätzlich gilt, dass die Handschriften des 17.-19. Jhs. nich mehr sehr sorgfältig aufgezeichnet sind. In der Themenauswahl und der Zusammenstellung der Texte kann man kein System erkennen, wie es im Mittelalter und der frühen Neuzeit der Fall war. Im Mittelalter stellten die schreibenden Mönche Werke nach einem bestimmten Plan zusammen, hier sind aber Laien und Privatleute tätig, die scheinbar ohne Systematik alles zusammentrugen, was sie interessierte und wessen sie habhaft werden konnten."*
> *(In essence, the manuscripts of the 17th-19th centuries were no longer carefully recorded. In the selection of topics and in the composition, one cannot recognise any system of the kind one finds in the Middle Ages and the Early Modern Period. In the Middle Ages, the monastic scribes composed works according to a certain plan, but here we have laymen and individuals at work who apparently unsystematically compiled everything which interested them, and which they could lay their hands on.[65])*

The later 'books of magic' from 1700 CE onward - and some earlier ones - were clearly not written by genuine magicians at all, but by well-meaning antiquarians who had the leisure and financial means to collect and transcribe older manuscripts My opinion is that, at some stage, a confusion arose and that *málrúnir* was taken to mean 'cryptic characters'.

Kennings

As previously stated, 'málrún' characters are sometimes accompanied by 'kennings' relating to the Futhark runes.

---

64 Bauer, Alessa "Die späten Runica Manuscripta aus Island. Was versteht man unter málrúnir?". Futhark: International Journal of Rune Studies, Vol. 1, 2010.
65 My translation.

These are metaphors which may be used to pad out the lore of the rune poems, but we need to use them which circumspection. Many of the translations I have seen are mystifying, and clearly need some deeper thought applied to them. Many of them can be found in the fragments from which the Old Icelandic Rune Poem was assembled[66], and these appear to have filtered down, frequently without discrimination and sometimes with rather thoughtless translation, until we see them appearing in the aforementioned "The Sorcerer's Screed". Remember that we are looking at copies of copies of copies, and that the original lists were compiled at a time when there was no standard spelling, and the Icelandic language still had dialects. An interesting feature, however, is that kennings appear for the runes which were added to the later, extended, Icelandic Futhark.

If you are interested enough to learn about the rune-kennings, I recommend reading "The Sorcerer's Screed" or Flowers' "Icelandic Magic"; to reproduce the tables again here would be superfluous. However, I would add some caveats regarding Skuggi's renditions and their respective translations into English, and will cover these according to the set (*kerfi*) in which they arise.

Set I

The kenning for the letter e, *Stunginn unnarhlemmur*, is rendered in English as "Stabbed Sea-Cover". This looks mystifying until one remembers that the e-phoneme was reintroduced to the row by adding an *Íss*-rune with a point or dot in the centre (ᛁ). Thus 'sea-cover' (ice) has been 'stabbed' by the point of the pen; that is all there is to it. This should be borne in mind whenever one sees the words 'stabbed', 'cracked', 'broken' or 'wounded' in the kennings for all the runes that were added again later.

---

66 See Page, R. I., "The Icelandic Rune Poem", Viking Society for Northern Research 1999

The kenning for the letter r, *Úlfalda-rás*, is rendered as 'Camel-Race'. Although the Icelandic word for 'camel' is undoubtedly *úlfaldi*, this is mystifying: I think it unlikely that mediaeval Icelanders would have heard of a camel, let alone seen one. My opinion is that it is a corruption of *úlfaldar*, 'of the wolf-age', which would make a connection with the Völuspá and Ragnarök.

The kenning for the letter þ is given by Skuggi as *Kvenna-ból*, and this has been translated as 'Women's Bed'. I think it quite obvious that Skuggi should have written *Kvenna-böl*, which would translate as 'Women's bale' and thereby be in accordance with the lore of the Younger Futhark.

Set II

The kenning for the letter o, *Valhallar-vísir*, is translated as 'King of Valhöll'. I have no idea why *vísir* has been translated as 'King', because it actually means 'pointer', like a signpost or the hands of a clock.

The kenning for the letter þ, *Raumur*, is translated as 'Hulk'. I could not find the word *raumur* in the modern Icelandic-English dictionary, but *raumr* appears in Zoega's "A Concise Dictionary of Old Icelandic" and is translated as 'a big and ugly person', tying in nicely with the concept of a giant.

Set IV

The kenning for the letter þ is given by Skuggi as *Fornjótur*, and this word is left untranslated in "The Sorcerer's Screed". I think it obvious that it should have read *Fornjötun*, 'Ancient Giant'.

Set V

The kenning for the letter r is given by Skuggi as *Snúðug för*, and this has been translated as 'Wild-Goose Chase'. I cannot imagine how they arrived at this translation, as it clearly translates as 'Swift Journey'.

Do the kennings have any real relationship with the unorthodox rune-rows that accompany them? This is difficult to tell. One has only to look at the Huld manuscript to see that many unorthodox rune-rows were designated as 'málrúnir', which makes it hard to define what a 'málrún' actually is. Without a doubt, however, plenty of the kennings in Skuggi's lists correspond with the elder lore, so that we can be fairly sure that they also correspond to the Younger Futhark. Do the rows and the kennings have any practical use for modern magicians in the Northern Tradition? I would suggest that the rows might be used to encrypt your intentions when composing spells, but you would first have to thoroughly familiarise yourself with a particular row until its use became second nature to you. The kennings are often useful to pad out our knowledge of the elder lore, and are worth meditating on, but please bear in mind the above admonitions. They have been unthinkingly copied over many generations, and errors have crept in.

APPENDIX 4

A BRIEF GUIDE TO THE GODS, WIGHTS AND WORLDS

Óðinn/Odin/Wotan/Woden

The chief of the gods, Odin has many and varied attributes. His name means 'Raging One', which is derived from the concept of *óðr* (Old English *wōd*), a state of divine ecstasy that can bring battle-frenzy or poetic inspiration. He was born of the union between the proto-god Borr and the giantess Bestla, together with his brothers Vili and Vé. Together, the three brothers slew the giant Ymir and, from his body, created heaven and earth. Though sometimes considered a god of war, Odin is better known for his restless search for knowledge, in which he frequently travels in disguise. He should usually be pictured as a middle-aged, one-eyed man wearing a cloak and a broad-brimmed hat. He rides an eight-legged steed named Sleipnir and carries a spear named Gungnir, and he is often accompanied by two wolves, Geri and Freki. He also has two ravens, Huginn and Muninn, who bring him news from all over the world.

Odin may be called upon for all acts of magic, for inspiration in writing and poetry, for communication, and for help in learning languages.

Þórr/Thor/Thunor

The son of Odin by his first consort, Jörð (Earth), Thor is a god of tremendous physical strength, and a match for most giants. He is a storm-god and is associated with thunder and lightning, riding the sky in a chariot drawn by two goats. Thor has a dwarf-forged hammer named Mjölnir, which he uses as a weapon to defend Asgard and Midgard against the race of giants. The hammer is also used in the myths to raise his goats from the dead (after being slain and eaten) and to hallow marriages. Thor is quick-tempered and has little time for subtlety or diplomacy. These attributes of strength and straight talk made him a favourite among the farmers of pre-Christian Iceland. He should be pictured as a huge, immensely strong man with flaming red hair and beard.

Thor may be called upon for matters requiring strength and endurance, for defence against enemies, and for the blessing of marriages.

Frey/Freyr/Ingvi

Unlike Odin and Thor, who are of the race of the Aesir, Frey is of another race of gods called the Vanir. He came to live among the Aesir with his father, Niord, and sister, Freya, when hostages were exchanged to seal the peace at the end of the primaeval war between the Aesir and Vanir. Frey was given the realm of Liosalfheim (Light-Elf-Home) to rule over, and therefore has a strong connection with the fair Elves. The name Frey actually means 'Lord', and he is also known as Ingvi, or Ing. Frey mainly rules over organic growth, sending the rain and sunshine that are needed to grow crops. Often depicted as priapic, he is the god of male fertility. One thing that stands out about Frey is that he is the only god who genuinely falls in love (as opposed to lust). He also owns a magical wild boar named Gullinbursti, which means 'Golden Bristles'. He should be depicted as a young, handsome and athletic man bearing an antler as a weapon.

Frey may be called upon for peace, prosperity, male fertility and male love-suits.

Týr/Tir/Tiu

Týr is best known in northern mythology for bravely stepping up and giving his hand as a pledge when the wolf Fenrir was to be bound. Fenrir did not trust the Aesir and their magical, dwarf-made fetter, and asked for one of them to place a hand in his mouth as a token of good faith. The wolf was bound, and Týr lost his hand. Týr is noted for his bravery and wisdom, and is also associated with the dispensation of justice and the outcome of wars, as trials by combat. Being one-handed, he cannot give an even-handed settlement; for amicable settlements in which both parties come away satisfied, it is better to appeal to Forseti. Týr may originally have been the chief of gods, for his name is cognate with Zeus, Jupiter and other Indo-European sky-gods. He should be pictured as a stern, rather saturnine man dressed in dark red robes.

Týr may be called upon for bravery and wisdom, for justice, and for victory in martial combat. However, you should be very sure of your case, because he will come down heavily on one side or the other.

Frigg/Frige/Frija

The goddess Frigg is the consort of Odin. She is a very motherly, protective goddess, and is the matron of the home, childbirth and women's affairs. Like the Norns, she is a weaver of fate, and her symbol is the distaff. It is said that she can foresee the future, but never tells of what she knows. She may be pictured as a middle-aged, matronly type, seated and spinning with a drop-spindle.

Frigg and her numerous handmaidens are good to call upon for all domestic matters, for healing, for protection and for marriage-oaths.

Freya/Freyja

Freya, the Lady of the Vanir, is the sister of Frey (Freyr) and the daughter of Niord. She is highly proficient in the magical arts and is said to have taught the art of seið to Odin. She also has associations with war, for Odin chooses half of the battle-slain, and she chooses the other half. Freya loves bright jewellery and is said to be beautiful and sexually promiscuous, the northern version of Venus. She drives a chariot drawn by cats, which might make her a favourite deity for anyone who has to chair a committee! Freya should be pictured as a beautiful, fair, young woman wearing a cloak of hawk-feathers. She may be called upon in matters of fertility, sexual love, and magic (particularly women's magic).

These are the principal deities, but there are many others, each with specific attributes, who govern certain aspects of earthly life. A good guide to them may be found in "Our Troth", Volume 1 (see bibliography).

Aesir

The Aesir are one of the two races of gods in the northern pantheon. Though the origins of some of them are shadowy, Odin is their chief. Odin, together with his brothers Vili (will) and Vé (holiness), is the hybrid offspring of an Etin-wife named Bestla and a strain that was somehow altogether different. The Aesir are therefore related to the Etins, so there is something of a family feud going on. On the whole, I see the Aesir as representing the principles of consciousness, discernment, distinction, and cosmic order.

Vanir

We know little of the Vanir or of their realm (Vanaheim). They are the other race of gods, and are said to have waged war against the Aesir in a distant time before humans even came into being. In that war, they were triumphant, and the Aesir sued for peace and the exchange of hostages. In this exchange, Niord (Njörðr) came to live among the Aesir together with Frey, his son, and Freya, his daughter. I see the Vanir as the agents of fertility and superabundant, organic growth - growth which must be held in check by the Etins.

Dark Elves or Dwarfs (Svartálfar)

The dark elves are older than the race of men, having been spontaneously generated from the rotting flesh of Ymir. They mainly dwell in a subterranean world named Svartalfheim and cannot endure sunlight. They are great smiths, being able to magically forge many wonderful artefacts. Sometimes they are inclined to be greedy, malign, or even murderous.

Light (or Fair) Elves (Ljósalfar)

Less is said of the light elves than of the dark elves in the Eddas. They appear to dwell in a bright, shining home above Midgard, and to have an affinity with the Vanir, as their home was given to Frey as a tooth-gift. I consider them (and this is a very personal view) to be associated with music, the arts, and the pleasant things in life which raise us above mere functional existence.

Etins (Jötnar)

The first race of beings to emerge after the 'big bang' from the meeting of primaeval fire and ice, they are usually depicted in the Eddas as gigantic, uncouth and greedy. On the other hand, they are also portrayed as having ancient, arcane wisdom which Odin avidly seeks to gain in contests of wit. They are by nature inimical to the Aesir and thus to their creation, mankind. I view them as the natural forces of destruction, which are allowed to hold sway in the autumn and winter but can also invade our lives at any given moment. After all, growth must be matched by destruction if the balance is to be maintained, just as the judicious gardener prunes his trees and eliminates weeds.

Thurses

Unfortunately, no hard-and-fast distinction can be made between Thurses and Etins on the basis of the lore which has been handed down to us. The terms are often used interchangeably. However, I view Thurses as hard-core frost-giants who are devoid of the wisdom of the Etins. They are agents of pure, icy destruction, who held sway when the ice-sheets covered northern Europe but have since retreated to the remaining glaciers and the 'absolute zero' of outer space.

Asgard (Ásgarðr)

The main dwelling place of the Aesir. It has many mansions, and you should refer to the Prose Edda for more details of these.

Vanaheim (Vanaheimr)

The home of the Vanir, or Wanes. I see this as lying to the west, across the sea, but little is known of it.

Liosalfheim (Ljósálfheimr)

Liosalfheim is the celestial home of the Light Elves.

Svartalfheim (Svartálfheimr)

The twilight, subterranean world of the Dark Elves.

Jotunheim (Jötunheimr)

The home of the Etins, somewhere to the east of Midgard.

Hel

The sleepy realm of the dead, ruled over by an Etin (daughter of Loki) of the same name. Most of us go there in the end, unless we distinguish ourselves in battle or by some other feats. I see this as a transit-station for true magicians.

Midgard (Miðgarðr)

The world of men. The entire physical plane, encompassing all of physical existence and ruled by time and the laws of physics.

Muspelsheim (Muspelsheimr)

The intensely bright, fiery world of primal Fire. No beings live there; at least none with which we can communicate.

Niflheim (Niflheimr)

The freezing, primal world which formed the counterpart of Muspelsheim at the beginning of all things. Again, nothing lives there with which we can communicate.

APPENDIX 5

A SELECT COMPENDIUM OF TRADITIONAL ICELANDIC SPELLS

The following spells have been selected from original books of magic on the basis of practicability, relevance to the modern reader, and the presence of a *galdrastafur* in the spell. If you decide to try these out, please do so with caution and remember that a spell sent injudiciously can come back to bite you! The staves have been copied anew, and the translations of the original instructions are, by and large, my own.

1. To soothe anger. If a person wants to still the anger of his enemy, let him carve this stave on oak and keep it in the palm of the left hand. (From Lbs 2413 8vo, no. 109)

2. To have friendship. Carve this in the right palm with spittle using the left ring finger while fasting. (From Lbs 2413 8vo, no. 96)

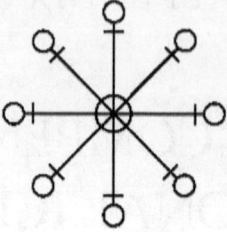

3. To win in disputes. Make this stave on yourself under your left arm* and you will have victory in disputes. (*I take this to mean on the inside of your left arm, otherwise it is physically nearly impossible.) (From Lbs 2413 8vo, no. 52)

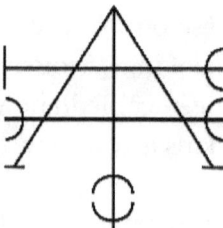

4. To know who has stolen from you. If you want to know who has stolen from you, carve this sign in the bottom of a bowl, fill it with water and add finely-ground yarrow to the water. Then say:

> "I desire, by the nature of the herb and the power of the sign, that I may see the shadow of the one who has stolen from me and others."

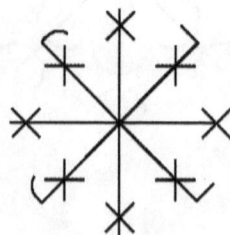

5. That people will love you. Carve this stave on your headgear while fasting, using the edge of a silver coin and your spittle. (From Lbs 2413 8vo, no. 94)

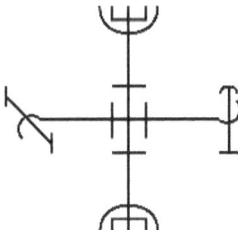

6. To win a girl's love. While fasting, make this sign with spittle in the palm of your right hand when you greet the girl whom you desire. (I take this to mean that you should trace the stave and then shake hands with her.) (From ATA, Amb 2, F 16:26 'Isländska Svartkonstboken', which Flowers refers to as 'The Galdrabók')

7. To win a girl's love. Carve [this stave] on cheese or bread with your eating-knife and feed her this stave. Have strong faith. (From Lbs 2413 8vo, no. 14)

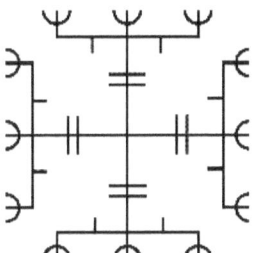

8. For successful fishing. To fish, carve this stave on your sinker. (From Lbs 2413 8vo, no. 28)

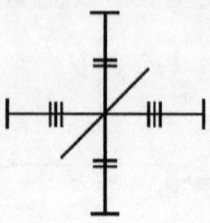

9. To win in trading. Keep this stave in your hand. (From Lbs 2413 8vo, no. 32)

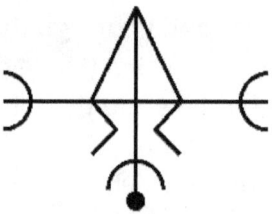

10. Bargain-sealer (Kaupaloki). Carve this stave on a slip of beechwood and carry it on the centre of your chest. (From ÍB 383 4to 'Huld', no. V)

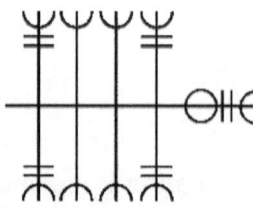

11. Luck-knot. This is a man's luck-knot, which he should always carry on him. (From Lbs 5472-1 4to, no. 19)

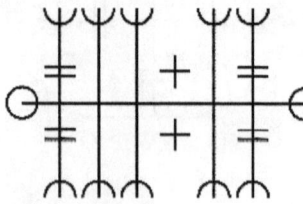

12. Signpost (Vegvisir). Carry this stave on you and you will not get lost in storms or bad weather, even though in unfamiliar surroundings.

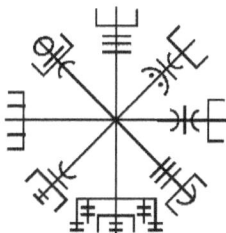

13. To get the thing you crave. Carve this stave on lead and keep in one of your hands. Carve with your eating knife and read this verse: *Da nobis Hodied dimi timi ej Petoribus men Indúcas.* (Note: these are corrupt and fragmented words from the Latin Lord's Prayer.) (From Lbs 2413 8vo, no. 34)

14. To win debates. Carve this stave with spittle while fasting and put under your left hand if you want to win debates. (From Lbs 2413 8vo, no. 69)

15. To hide an object. If you want to hide something so it shall not be found, carve this stave on it with your eating knife and it will not be found. Say Pater Noster. (From Lbs 2413 8vo, no. 73)

16. Against an evil spirit. If an evil spirit is around, carve this stave over the door of your house. Make an awl of juniper or silver. (From Lbs 2413 8vo, no. 130)

17. To inflict intolerable farting. Carve on oak with a human finger-bone or an unused knife. Smear with your blood and read this: "I carve you 8 Ases, 9 Needs and 13 Thurses. You shall explode to great discomfort. I forbid your backside to fall apart. Now shit or burst." This should be done with a full moon. (From Lbs 2413 8vo, no. 67)

ppppppppp
ſſſſſſſſſſſſſſ
qqqqqqqq

18. To make an enemy fear you. Carve this stave on lead with your eating knife and carry it under your left arm. (From Lbs 2413 8vo, no. 57)

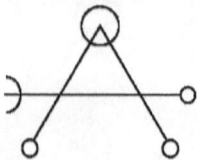

19. To win at gaming. If you want to win at gaming, carve this stave on your palm using your finger and your spittle. (From Lbs 2413 8vo, no. 136)

20. To keep a person away from your house. If you want a certain person to stay away from your home, carve this stave on rowan wood when the sun is at its zenith, and walk 3 times sun-wise and 3 time widdershins around your house, and hold on to the rowan stick and a thistle, then put both of them up over the centre of your door. (From ATA, Amb 2, F 16:26 'Isländska Svartkonstboken')

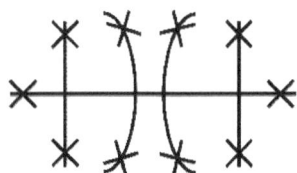

21. Against fear. Whosoever carries these staves on himself will fear neither dead nor living things.

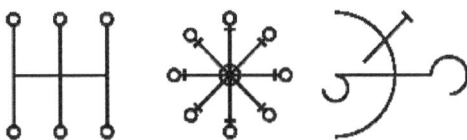

22. To dream what you will. Write these staves on brass and lay on your ear before you sleep, and you will know what you wish to know.

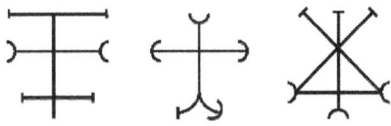

23. Against fart-runes. Carve these staves to counter farting spells that have been cast. (From Lbs 2413 8vo, no. 75)

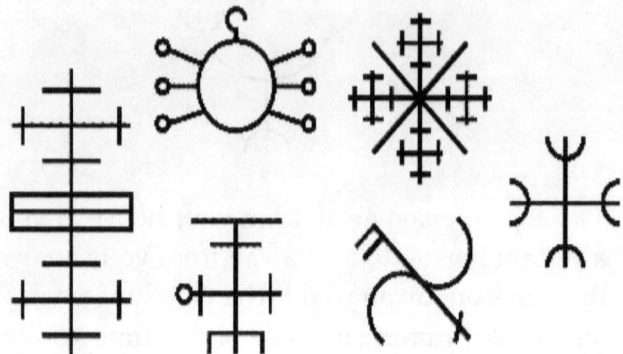

24. Whetting staves. These are to help when whetting your scythe or knife. Carve the upper stave on top of your whetstone, the lower one underneath. Then place grass over the whetstone for a while. Then, when you sharpen, face away from the sun and do not look at the cutting edge. (From ÍB 383 4to 'Huld', no. VI)

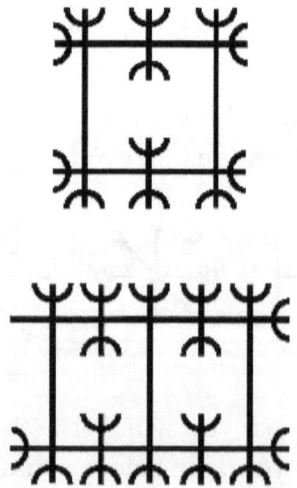

25. To heal sick livestock (Mary's Cross). Let this stave be placed above and under livestock which ails in some way. (From Lbs 764 8vo, no. 47)

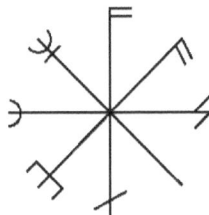

26. So that nothing may be stolen from your house. Carve this stave on the door-post of the house and make a cross over it with the wrong hand. (From Lbs 764 8vo, no. 32)

27. Against imprecations. Write this sigil on sanctified paper and carry it on your chest. (From Lbs 2413 8vo, no. 144)

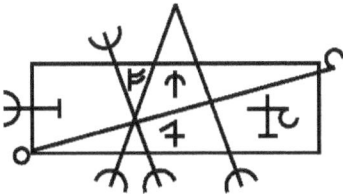

28. To summon a northerly blizzard. Carve this stave on the head of a ling (fish) and walk northward while waving it in the air. (From Lbs 2413 8vo, no. 126)

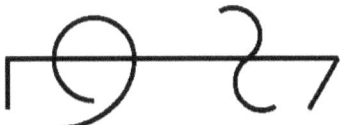

29. To focus the mind. Bear these staves on the left side of your chest to focus the mind. (From ÍB 383 4to 'Huld', no. XXX)

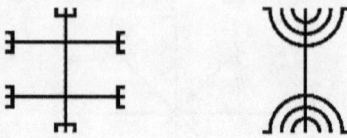

30. Against melancholy. Carry these symbols on your breast. (From Lbs 143 8vo, no. 7)

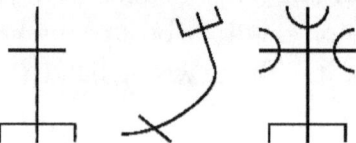

31. Protection against evil visitations of wicked men. One shall bear the following symbols. (From Lbs 143 8vo, no. 6)

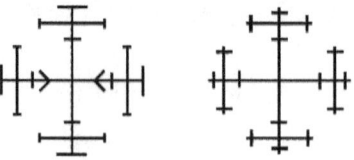

32. To know what is hidden to the common man. Carve these staves on brass with iron, and sleep with them close to your ear. You will experience.

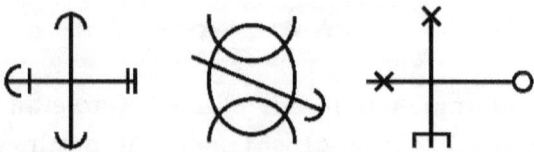

BIBLIOGRAPHY

Anon.: Lbs 2413 8vo, National and University Library of Iceland, Reykjavík, 1800

Anon.: Lbs 764 8vo, National and University Library of Iceland, Reykjavík, 1820

Anon.: AM 434 a 12mo 'Lækningakver', Arnamagnaean Inst. Denmark, Copenhagen, 1475-1525

Anon.: ATA, Amb 2, F 16:26 'Galdrabók', Antiquarian Topical Archive, Stockholm, 1550-1650

Anon.: Lbs 143 8vo 'Galdrakver', National and University Library of Iceland, Reykjavík, 1670/2004

Aswynn, Freya: "Leaves of Yggdrasil". BM Aswynn, London, 1988

Bates, Brian: "The Way of Wyrd". Hay House, London, 2012

Bauer, Alessa: "Die späten Runica Manuscripta aus Island". International Journal of Rune Studies, 2010

Bauschatz, Paul C.: "The Well and the Tree". University of Massachusetts, Boston, 1982

Branston, Brian: "The Lost Gods of England". Thames & Hudson, London, 1974

Crowfoot, Greg: "Understanding the Galdrabók". Internet, 1996

Cunningham, David Michael et al.: "Creating Magickal Entities". Egregore Publishing, Perrysburg, OH, USA, 2003

Davies, Owen: "Grimoires. A History of Magic Books". OUP, Oxford, 2009

Dilmann, Francois-Xavier: "Les magiciens dans l'Islande Ancienne". Gustav Adolfs Akademien, Uppsala: 2006

Einar Ólafur Sveinsson: "The Folk-Stories of Iceland". Viking Society for Northern Research, London, 2003

Flowers, Stephen E.: "The Galdrabók". Runa-Raven Press, Smithville, TX, USA, 2005

Flowers, Stephen E.: "Icelandic Magic: Practical secrets of the northern grimoires". Inner Traditions, Rochester, Vermont, USA, 2016

Fry, Stephen: "The Ode Less Travelled". Arrow Books, London, 2007

Geir Vigfússon: ÍB 383 4to 'Huld', National and University Library of Iceland, 1860

Gísli Sigurðsson and Vésteinn Ólason, eds.: "The Manuscripts of Iceland". Árni Magnússon Institute, Reykjavík, 2004

Greer, John Michael: "Circles of Power". Llewellyn, Minnesota, USA, 1997

Gundarsson, Kveldulf: "Elves, Wights, and Trolls". iUniverse, Lincoln, Nebraska, USA, 2007

Hastrup, Kirsten: "Iceland: Sorcerers and Paganism". OUP, Oxford, 1990

Hine, Phil: "Condensed Chaos: An Introduction to Chaos Magic". New Falcon Publications, Tempe, Arizona, USA, 1995

Hollander, Lee M. (Transl.): "The Poetic Edda". University of Texas Press,

Austin, TX, USA, 1962

Jón Ólafsson úr Grunnavík: AM 413 fol. 'Runologia', Arnamagnaean Inst. Denmark, Copenhagen, 1752

Jón R. Hjálmarsson: "History of Iceland". Forlagið, Reykjavík, 2009

Kelly, Michael: "The Book of Ogham". CreateSpace Independent Publishing Platform, 2014

Kieckhefer, Richard: "Magic in the Middle Ages". Cambridge University Press, Cambridge, 1989

Lecouteux, Claude: "The Tradition of Household Spirits". Inner Traditions, Rochester, Vermont, USA, 2013

Lee, Dave: "Bright from the Well". Mandrake, Oxford, 2008

MacLeod, Mindy & Mees, Bernard: "Runic Amulets and Magic Objects". The Boydell Press, Woodbridge, UK, 2006

Magnús Rafnsson: "Angurgapi: The Witch-hunts in Iceland". Strandagaldur, Hólmavík, Iceland, 2003

Magnús Rafnsson (Ed.): "Rún". Strandagaldur, Hólmavík, Iceland, 2014

Magnús Rafnsson (Ed.): "Tvær galdraskræður". Strandagaldur, Hólmavík, Iceland, 2008

Margaret Clunies Ross, ed.: "Old Icelandic Literature and Society". Cambridge University Press, Cambridge, 2000

May & Hallberg Hallmundsson: "Icelandic Folk and Fairy Tales". Forlagið, Reykjavík, 2009

Mees, Bernard: "The Yew Rune, Yogh and Yew". Leeds Studies in English, New Series XLII, University of Leeds, Leeds, 2011

Mitchell, Stephen A.: "The Whetstone a Symbol of Authority in Old English and Old Norse". www.academia.edu, 1985

Mitchell, Stephen A.: "Witchcraft and Magic in the Nordic Middle Ages". University of Pennsylvania Press, Philadelphia, 2011

Ólafur Davíðsson: "Islaendische Zauberzeichen und Zauberbuecher". Zeitschrift des vereins fuer Volkskunde, Berlin, 1903

Page, R. I.: "The Icelandic Rune Poem". Viking Society for Northern Research, 1999

Page, R. I.: "Runes". The British Museum Press, London, 2007

Pennick, Nigel: "Pagan Magic of the Northern Tradition". Destiny Books, Rochester, Vermont, USA, 2015

Simpson, Jacqueline: "Icelandic Folktales and Legends". B.T. Batsford Ltd, London, 1972

Skuggi (Jochum Eggertsson): "Galdraskræða". Reykjavík, 1940 (translated into English as "Sorcerer's Screed", Lesstofan, Reykjavík, 2015)

Smith, Christopher A.: "The Icelandic Tradition of Magic: Analysis of a Late Eighteenth-Century Icelandic Galdrabók". Numen Books, 2012

Smith, Christopher A.: "Icelandic Magic: Aims, tools and techniques of the Icelandic sorcerers". Avalonia, London, 2015

Sturluson, Snorri: "Heimskringla". Dover edition, New York, 1990

Sturluson, Snorri: "Edda". Dent, London, 1987

The Troth: "Our Troth, Volume I". The Troth, North Charleston, SC, USA,

2006 (2nd Edition)

Thorsson, Edred: "Futhark: A Handbook of Rune Magic". Weiser, York Beach, Maine, USA, 1984

Thorsson, Edred: "Rune-Song". Runa-Raven Press, Austin, Texas, 1993

Thorsson, Edred: "ALU: An Advanced Guide to Operative Runology". Weiser, San Francisco, 2012

Thorsson, Edred: "Runelore". Weiser, York Beach, Maine, USA, 1987

Thorsson, Edred: "Northern Magic". Llewellyn, St. Paul, NM, USA, 1998 (2nd edition)

Thorsson, Edred: "At the Well of Wyrd". Weiser, York Beach, Maine, USA, 1988

Thorsson, Edred: "The Nine Doors of Midgard". The Rune-Gild, South Burlington, VT, USA, 2016

Viking Society for Northern Research: "Three Icelandic Outlaw Sagas". VSNR, London, 2004

INDEX

A

Aesir....... 16, 17, 52, 73, 75, 84, 85, 111, 123, 126, 127, 135, 169, 182, 192, 227, 228, 229, 230, 231
Ansuz..............51, 52, 75, 136, 213
Asgard17, 51, 52, 74, 106, 111, 112, 114, 115, 145, 169, 192, 227, 231
Auðumla.............................. 15, 49

B

Baldur 17, 106, 123
Berkano..........................76, 84, 213
bindrune 83, 95, 130, 131, 132, 133, 134, 136, 141, 152, 157, 160, 178, 183, 201
blood......15, 17, 39, 52, 70, 82, 123, 127, 134, 135, 155, 180, 183, 201, 238

C

candles 99, 101, 111, 115, 118, 167, 203, 205, 206
carving.... 45, 93, 99, 133, 134, 149, 155, 158
Claude Lecouteux 124
Colin Wilson......................... 13, 14
colour...39, 40, 42, 90, 91, 107, 110, 130, 134, 135, 160, 172, 176
colouring.............................93, 134

D

Dagaz............. 85, 86, 193, 212, 213
Daily Assertion.................... 30, 31
Dark Elves...........15, 192, 230, 231

divination 13, 52, 64, 70, 83, 84, 90, 92, 104, 105, 116, 118, 162, 164, 186, 188, 189, 190, 193

E

Edred Thorsson.. 46, 60, 68, 71, 96, 116, 130, 135, 143, 146, 148, 170, 193, 210
Ehwaz......................77, 78, 79, 213
Eihwaz.....................65, 66, 68, 213
Elhaz 51, 54, 70, 71, 83, 95, 131, 213
Etin 15, 74, 82, 85, 229, 231

F

Fehu 46, 47, 55, 62, 87, 90, 91, 130, 131, 133, 136, 156, 193, 213
Flowers, Dr Stephen E.. 8, 68, 116, 143, 144, 146, 147, 148, 149, 210, 219, 223, 235, 243
Frau Holle 60, 77, 181
Frey.. 65, 83, 85, 106, 126, 170, 227, 229, 230
Freya......60, 84, 123, 126, 163, 227, 229, 230, 243
Freya Aswynn............................60
Frigg 126, 134, 228
Futhark....43, 44, 45, 46, 52, 55, 59, 60, 61, 65, 66, 67, 68, 71, 73, 81, 87, 92, 96, 116, 130, 131, 132, 135, 139, 140, 141, 143, 149, 152, 190, 201, 212, 214, 216, 218, 221, 222, 224, 225, 245
Futhorc.........45, 55, 61, 66, 81, 214

G

Galdor..... 46, 47, 91, 128, 130, 201, 202
   galdor...50, 51, 52, 54, 56, 57, 59, 61, 63, 64, 66, 68, 70, 72, 73, 76, 77, 79, 81, 83, 85, 86, 87
galdramyndir 121, 138, 152
galdrastafir 8, 45, 121, 135, 138, 139, 143, 144, 145, 146, 149, 150, 152, 178, 189, 207
galdrastafur 121, 141, 142, 149, 160, 202, 233
Gebo............... 56, 91, 132, 133, 213
Geir Vigfússon 141, 243
Ginnungagap......14, 28, 31, 44, 64, 169

H

Hagalaz 59, 60, 61, 77, 91, 132, 213
harrow 110, 111, 113, 117, 165, 169, 203
Heimdall.............................. 17, 18
Hel 145, 192, 231
Helm of Awe 143, 148, 194, 195, 196, 197, 198
Huld...141, 142, 144, 158, 225, 236, 240, 242, 243

I

incantation 121, 127, 128, 129, 130, 148, 153, 158, 160, 179, 180, 201, 203
incense.99, 102, 105, 106, 111, 112, 113, 115, 118, 126, 167, 179, 183, 203, 205, 206
Ingwaz 83, 213
Isa62, 63, 64, 72, 83, 132, 159, 213

J

Jera..64, 65, 66, 72, 84, 91, 130, 213
Jochum Eggertsson .. 141, 219, 244
Jotunheim 145, 192, 231

Justin Foster 143, 146, 149

K

Kenaz.....54, 55, 101, 112, 115, 201, 213
kennings......18, 45, 46, 65, 83, 140, 219, 222, 223, 225
Kvasir 17, 135, 201, 204
Kveldulf Gundarsson 124

L

Laguz........................... 81, 82, 213
Lammas.....................................165
liminality 86, 168
Liosalfheim ..84, 145, 192, 227, 231

M

magical diary 30, 35, 38, 39, 40, 97, 98, 100, 118
málrúnir 219, 220, 221, 222, 225
Máni 72, 126, 164
Mannaz........................79, 133, 213
mead.... 17, 127, 135, 200, 201, 203, 205
Mead............................... 17, 19, 52
Meditation............................32, 33
Michael Kelly 26
Midgard 15, 51, 80, 81, 106, 114, 115, 116, 145, 169, 192, 210, 227, 230, 231, 232
Midsummer's Eve................8, 161
Mimir...................................16, 52
Mjölnir............... 113, 114, 115, 227
Moon ... 24, 104, 110, 161, 163, 164, 182
Muspelsheim.... 14, 47, 64, 82, 145, 169, 192, 232

N

narrative......14, 26, 27, 28, 31, 116, 128, 151, 167, 179, 201
Nauðiz................. 61, 101, 115, 213

Niflheim.. 14, 64, 82, 145, 192, 193, 232
Norns 26, 69, 70, 126, 228

O

Odin...14, 15, 16, 17, 29, 44, 49, 51, 52, 60, 71, 75, 89, 106, 112, 114, 118, 123, 126, 127, 141, 163, 179, 182, 197, 200, 201, 203, 204, 226, 227, 228, 229, 230
Othala .86, 90, 91, 95, 133, 212, 213

P

pentimal number system 142, 143
Perthro 68, 70, 91, 213
pigment............................134, 135

R

Raiðo..53, 54, 62, 79, 108, 131, 156, 213
Rig................. 14, 17, 18, 23, 43, 87
ritual 26, 53, 54, 79, 96, 99, 101, 108, 109, 110, 111, 114, 115, 116, 117, 118, 127, 128, 159, 160, 196, 197, 203, 206
Rúna........................... 29, 126, 208

S

scrying 103, 105, 187, 188
seasons........................ 65, 164, 166
Sending..... 171, 174, 175, 176, 177, 178, 179, 180, 181, 182, 183
Snorri Sturluson 14, 75, 220
Sowilo 72, 73, 133, 213
spittle ...93, 132, 135, 155, 156, 159, 207, 234, 235, 237, 239
stead.....61, 110, 111, 113, 114, 115, 118, 154, 166, 167, 169, 183, 203, 204, 206
Sun.72, 73, 161, 163, 164, 213, 215, 217

Sunna................... 72, 126, 164, 169
Svartalfheim.15, 145, 192, 230, 231

T

talisman 72, 84, 111, 116, 131, 132, 150, 154, 159, 200, 203, 204, 205, 206
Thor 51, 52, 106, 113, 114, 115, 123, 126, 163, 226, 227
Thurisaz 50, 51, 94, 159, 213
Tiwaz.....................73, 75, 132, 213
tools. 8, 11, 36, 43, 94, 99, 100, 105, 109, 156, 167, 206, 244
Týr 73, 74, 75, 76, 126, 140, 156, 163, 167, 217, 228

U

Uruz..........................48, 49, 91, 213

V

Vanaheim...145, 170, 192, 229, 231
visualisation 37, 41, 91, 94, 99, 113, 134, 158, 167, 181, 196, 198, 206

W

washing........96, 107, 196, 197, 198
wealth.. 12, 46, 47, 55, 87, 130, 131, 197, 213
wights 113, 115, 117, 124, 127, 167, 181
Wunjo 57, 91, 95, 130, 133, 213
Wyrd . 26, 61, 69, 70, 167, 193, 243, 245

Y

yarrow......................104, 187, 234
Yggdrasil.....16, 44, 60, 67, 80, 110, 145, 146, 170, 192, 243
Ymir......................15, 49, 226, 230

FROM THE SAME AUTHOR

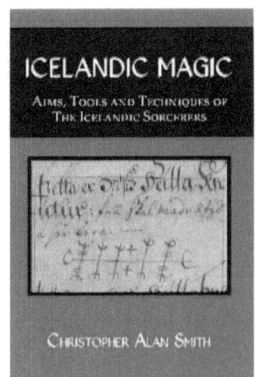

Icelandic Magic:
Aims, tools and techniques of the Icelandic sorcerers

By Christopher Alan Smith

This unprecedented work meticulously studies no less than 6 original Icelandic manuscripts dating from 1500 to 1860 to extract a picture of the aims, tools and techniques of Icelandic sorcerers.

Available in paperback, hardback and kindle editions.

WWW.AVALONIABOOKS.COM

www.ingramcontent.com/pod-product-compliance
Lightning Source LLC
Chambersburg PA
CBHW020649230426

43665CB00008B/364